6-5-75

Drugs on the Market

Drugs on the Market

The Impact of Public Policy
on the Retail Market for
Prescription Drugs

John F. Cady
University of Arizona

Lexington Books
D.C. Heath and Company
Lexington, Massachusetts
Toronto   London

Library of Congress Cataloging in Publication Data

Cady, John F.
   Drugs on the market.

   Bibliography: p.
   Includes index.
   1. Drug trade—United States. 2. Drugs—Laws and legislation—United
States. I. Title.
HD9666.6.C25   381'.45'61510973   74-21483
ISBN 0-669-96842-0

Published simultaneously in Canada.

Printed in the United States of America.

International Standard Book Number: 0-669-96842-0

Library of Congress Catalog Card Number: 74-21483

Contents

List of Figures

List of Tables

Preface

A major debt is owed to many individuals who have contributed to the development and conduct of this study. I would like to give special thanks to Dr. Lee E. Preston, State University of New York at Buffalo. Dr. Preston provided intellectual stimulation and guidance throughout this project, and suggested many fruitful areas of inquiry within the framework of the study.

Dr. Albert Wertheimer, Director of the Graduate Program in Pharmacy, University of Minnesota, rendered invaluable assistance in the formulative stages. It was Dr. Wertheimer who originally suggested to me the need for this study of regulatory impact in the retail market for prescription drugs.

Dr. Brian T. Ratchford and Dr. Perry Bliss, State University of New York at Buffalo, provided continuous review, criticism and encouragement.

This research would have been impossible to carry out had it not been for the interest and assistance of members of the industry. My sincere appreciation is expressed to Mr. Michael Zagorac of the National Association of Chain Drug Stores and Mr. James A. Donahue of Lea, Inc. These individuals made the survey data used in this study available to me.

Finally, special thanks are due to Dr. F. Marion Fletcher. It was Dr. Fletcher's pathbreaking study, *Market Restraints in the Retail Drug Industry*, which called attention to the potentially restrictive self-regulatory practices observed in the retail prescription drug market.

Despite the assistance and guidance received, any errors or omissions remaining are solely my responsibility.

1 Introduction

Prescription drug retailing is a regulated sector of our economy. As such it is the object of public policy explicitly enacted to promote the public welfare. The purpose of this study is to examine the economic effects of regulation of the retail market for prescription drugs. Specifically the study is designed to analyze this market with an aim toward answering three related questions:

What are the effects of public policy on the structure of the market? What are the effects of public policy on the conduct of competition in the market? What are the effects of market structure and competitive conduct on consumer prescription drug prices?

The motivation to carry out the research is found in the economic and socio-political relationship between this market and society at large.

Total expenditures for prescription drugs have increased markedly over the past several years from an estimated $3.3 billion in 1967 to $8 billion in 1973; current projections for 1975 indicate expenditures close to ten billion dollars.[1,2] While increased levels of expenditure have been accompanied by an increase in third party payment programs in both the private and public sectors, over 85 percent of prescription drug expenditures are borne by individual consumers.[3] The impact of these expenditures falls most heavily on the aged and the poor. Those over sixty-five have average prescription expenditures of almost three times those of individuals under sixty-five.[4] The compound effects of limited income and chronic illness, which characterize our elderly population, potentially lower the ability of the aged to receive adequate medical treatment.

... Their [the elderly] inordinate health needs, their high health costs in general and high drug costs in particular, and their limited financial resources combine to create a serious and sometimes devastating medical and economic problem far out of proportion to their numbers.[5]

Expressed political concern over the performance of the retail drug market may be witnessed at both federal and state levels. In an address before the Sherman Act Committee of the Antitrust Section of the American Bar Association, Roland Donnem, Director of Policy Planning for the Department of Justice commented,

In view of the alarming rate of recent increases in general health costs, which falls especially hard upon the elderly and the poor, it seems that sound economic and social policy dictate that any competitive restraints which have the effect of raising drug costs should be kept to the minimum required by considerations of

1

public safety. . . . While investigation may show specific laws or regulations to be justified by health and safety considerations [many regulations and laws in the retail drug market] seem to unduly interfere with competition.[6]

A similar stance was taken regarding this market by Caspar Weinberger as Chairman of the Federal Trade Commission.

In view of the rapidly rising costs of health care, the fact that the cost of drugs falls especially heavy on the aged and the poor, and the fact that Government health programs, most notably Medicare, are expanding rapidly, we must seek in every way possible to assure effective competition in this area.

Practices that reduce price competition in drugs are a detriment to the public welfare.[7]

Similar statements expressing concern for competition in this market have come from other executive branches,[8] and increasingly are heard in the halls of Congress.

. . . at a time of high unemployment and increasing health care costs for the American people, the drug industry is reaping astronomical profits. . . . It is certainly [an] over protected [industry] a situation that contributes strongly to its enormous profits. . . . Neither [drug manufacturers nor drug retailers] is willing to subordinate its profit making in behalf of lower drug prices to consumers.[9]

Congressman Rosenthal estimates that consumers pay over one billion dollars annually in unnecessary drug costs because of market competition impedimenta and accordingly has introduced several pieces of legislation aimed at increasing competition in both the production and distribution sectors of the market.[10]

At the state and local levels also, there is evidence of increased awareness of and concern for the state of retail competition and prescription drug prices. At least a dozen states and several major cities are currently examining the competitive conduct of the retail drug sector.[11,12,13,14] Further evidence of social concern over the performance of the sector, apart from that voiced by politicians and spokesmen for public agencies, is found in a number of articles and statements written by, and surveys sponsored by, consumer interest groups.[15,16,17,18]

Despite this concern, there has been no detailed study of the retail prescription drug market coincident with the growth in concern over the nature of competition and retail prices. Those studies that have been conducted are largely confined to price surveys in limited geographic areas, or detailed studies of a very small sample.[19,20,21]

It is my intent in this study to analyze the current status of competition and to describe and analyze the effects of current public policy on competition in this market. It is hoped that this endeavor will provide a basis for the assessment of the impact of current policy, and the development of future policy.

Chapter 2 discusses the public policy process in general and as specifically applied to the development and implementation of regulations in the retail market for prescription drugs. The framework for analysis of the economic effects of regulation is presented in this section.

Chapter 3 provides an overview of the retail prescription drug market. In this section the identification of significant trends in sales size of establishments, organization of establishments, and output composition of establishments is made.

Chapter 4 discusses the cost functions and the structure of costs in pharmacy retailing. The chapter considers the issues of scale economies and the impact of sales composition on pharmacy costs.

Chapter 5 estimates the direct impact of regulation on market structure. The effects of regulation on establishment sales size, output composition and organization are examined. The chapter presents an estimate of the costs of regulation resulting from an impact on market structure.

Chapters 6 and 7 examine competition in the market. In Chapter 6 the variations in the elements of competition among pharmacies are described. In Chapter 7 these variations are examined in a model of retail competition. This model explores the dimensions of competition which account for variations in total sales and prescription drug sales. The impact of regulations potentially restricting price competition is demonstrated by testing the model in regulated and unregulated states.

Chapter 8 estimates the effects of regulation on prescription drug prices independent of structurally related characteristics. This chapter concludes with an examination of the impact of regulation at retail on per capita prescription drug consumption.

Chapter 9 presents the summary findings of the study.

2 Public Policy and the Retail Market for Prescription Drugs

" 'Public policy' refers to deliberate action taken by various parts of a government in pursuit of certain *objectives*. This action takes the form of particular *instruments* which have definite *effects* in the face of current forces."[1] To this definition is added one essential characteristic of public policy—*process*.

The process of public policy is of particular significance in two respects. The process of *policy formation* determines how current social forces are channelled into objectives, and which of numerous and potentially conflicting objectives are pursued by social agencies.

The process of *policy implementation* determines the manner in which chosen objectives are pursued—through the use of what instruments.

In this chapter the objectives, processes, and instruments of public policy in the retail prescription drug market are discussed, and a framework for an analysis of the effects of public policy developed.

Figure 2-1 depicts the overall public policy process as a sequential and reiterative system. At any point in time policy decisionmakers are faced with multiple objectives to choose among. Limited resources allow only those objectives with the highest current priority to be pursued. Basically the current priority of objectives is influenced in two ways. The first force influencing the priority of objectives can be described as social pressure reflecting the collective desires of the system's public. "Generally one thinks of any outcome, including policy outcomes, as a result of forces brought to bear upon a system and causing it to make particular responses."[2] The second way in which the priority of objectives may be influenced comes about as a result of the functioning of the system itself. Once objectives are chosen and processes to attain them are developed, the success of those processes in the achievement of the objectives may alter the priority given those objectives in the future. If the processes implemented are successful and the objectives are attained, new objectives will replace those met. If the processes implemented are unsuccessful in meeting objectives or if unforeseen outcomes result from the implementation of specific processes, either processes or objectives may be modified until some acceptable balance between them is met.

In the following sections, the objectives and the process by which objectives are pursued regarding the distribution of drug products are analyzed. It will be shown that the priority of objectives originally chosen for consideration has changed over time. An illustration of the apparent inability of current measures

5

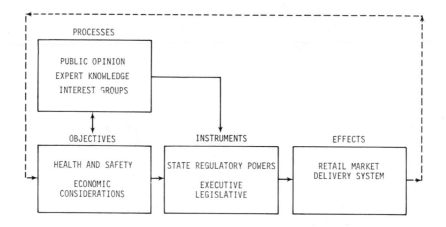

Figure 2-1. Public Policy Process in the Prescription Drug Market

to meet developing priorities of society relative to drug distribution provides a strong stimulus to the study of current policy effects.

Policy Objectives in the Prescription Drug Market

The primary stated objective of public policy regarding drug products, expressed at both federal and state levels, is the protection of the public health and safety. At the federal level the statement of these objectives may be traced to congressional debate preceding the enactment of the 1907 Pure Food and Drug Act.[3] The 1938 *Food, Drug and Cosmetic Act* strongly reiterated this concern over the sale and distribution of drug products and delegated the responsibility for regulating standards of quality, purity, and efficacy to the Food and Drug Administration.

The concerns for health and safety expressed at the federal level are primarily concerned with drug production. The enactment of policy consistent with federal provisions regarding the distribution and final sale of drug products is carried out by the state.

Statements of concern for public health and safety at the state level may be found in an examination of legislative provisions. Pennsylvania's statutes dealing with drug distribution, for example, state "[The purpose of all legislation and rule making is] designed to insure methods of operation and conduct which protect the public health, safety and welfare. . . ."[4] Similar objectives can be found on examination of the regulations dealing with drug distribution of virtually every state.[5] The wording of the Pennsylvania statutes (and that of most other states) is particularly significant. Provision for the protection of public health and safety is maintained through the regulation of the "operation and conduct" of drug distribution. Specific rule making and legislation potentially prescribe those who are to participate in the distribution of drug products and prescribe and proscribe the methods of distribution.[6]

Processes and Instruments

The retail distribution of prescription drugs is regulated at the state level through two mechanisms: pharmacy board regulation and legal statute. Before describing these instruments of regulation, consideration will be given to the development of both regulation and statute.

Pharmacy Regulation and Pharmacy Boards

State boards of pharmacy, in structure and function, are similar to other trade regulation agencies. Their primary function is occupational licensing, and they are created to assess the competence and insure continued competence of those engaged in a trade or profession. Aside from licensing, however, pharmacy boards are legislatively granted broad discretionary powers in the regulation of the profession of pharmacy and the conduct of retail trade in the sector.

Most of the state laws do not contain provisions that are concerned with the minutiae of retail drugstore operations, but rather (1) require registered pharmacists to dispense drugs, (2) specify registration requisites, (3) establish certain standards, and (4) empower the pharmacy boards to adopt the detailed rules necessary for administering the other enactments. The boards are also generally responsible for securing compliance with state drug adulteration laws and for promulgation and enforcement of rules to govern the practice of retail pharmacy.[7]

Pharmacy boards in all fifty states and the District of Columbia have the power to adopt and carry out regulations dealing with the retail pharmacy trade.

The pharmacy laws and rules of the various states give the boards a powerful weapon to force compliance with the provisions – license suspension and/or revocation. A pharmacist must be registered to practice his profession. Threat of revocation of his license is a menace to his livelihood, so he is apt to abide by the board's wishes. The same is true for a pharmacy, since it must be registered before it may open for business.[8]

Because of the power and legislatively granted means of control vested in state pharmacy boards, the regulations enacted by these boards have a potentially great effect on the manner in which trade is carried on in the sector.

Fletcher concludes that an examination of the membership patterns of state pharmacy boards contributes greatly to an explanation of the types of regulations effected by them.[9] Pharmacy boards are predominantly controlled by state pharmaceutical associations, which in turn are controlled by retail pharmacists (who comprise the largest segment of the pharmacist population). Within the retail pharmacist segment, the independent owner exerts the greatest control over the associations.

Basically there are three reasons why control has come to rest with the independent owner segment:

> One is that the economic issues that come within the domain of the boards of pharmacy are of the utmost importance to owners. ... [Independent] pharmacist entrepreneurs are acutely aware of the threat to their financial status that is created by chain and discount drugstore operations. The independents, accordingly, embrace legislative and regulatory policies that restrict the right of these types of outlets to enter the retail drug industry and limit the managerial prerogative of chains and discounters. ... A second reason for the dominance of retail owners over state pharmaceutical associations and hence state pharmacy boards is the failure of employee pharmacists to participate actively in association activities. ... A third factor ... facilitates control of state pharmaceutical associations by independent drugstore owners. ... In some states ... employee pharmacists ... [are] denied membership completely while nonpharmacist drugstore owners are accorded full membership privileges. ...[10]

The Development of Legal Statute

In the consideration of legislation regulating a specialized sector such as retail drug distribution, legislatures rely on three sources of guidance: public opinion, expert knowledge, and lobbying organizations. Historically, in the absence of major abuses, public opinion has had a small role in shaping the structure of retail drug legislation. Pharmacy boards have provided expert knowledge. The primary source of lobbying influence over state legislatures is found in the two major retailer organizations representing this sector.

The older and larger of these associations is the National Association of Retail Druggists (N.A.R.D.). N.A.R.D., in 1965, counted over 37,300 members, who owned and operated nearly 43,500 pharmacies. These pharmacies represented over 90 percent of the pharmacies in the United States in that year. By affiliate membership, all fifty state pharmaceutical associations also belong to N.A.R.D.[11]

N.A.R.D. has been recognized as, ". . . the politically most powerful of all retail trade associations . . . ,"[12] and has a long history of actively lobbying and campaigning for the economic interests of the independent pharmacist. It is primarily through the efforts of N.A.R.D., spanning forty years, that state resale price maintenance laws, the Miller-Tydings Act, and the McGuire Act were passed. Through the experience gained in lobbying for resale price maintenance N.A.R.D. has developed what can only be described as a highly efficient, powerful organization which has consistently pressed for the enactment of legislation in the interest of the independent pharmacist-owner.

The second principal trade association represented in the retail drug market is the National Association of Chain Drug Stores (N.A.C.D.S.), which in 1965 represented 127 drug chains ranging in size from three to 476 establishments. The chains represented by N.A.C.D.S. in that year operated approximately two-thirds of the nation's estimated 5,000 chain drugstores.[13] In contrast to the aggressive manner in which N.A.R.D. has pursued political-economic issues, N.A.C.D.S. has only recently become involved in these campaigns. Historically N.A.C.D.S.'s name has rarely been associated with the economic debates over retail pharmacy practices.

Regulation and Statute—
Instruments of Public Policy

As previously noted the regulations in effect in the retail drug market are of two types: legal statute and pharmacy board regulation. In this study no distinction is made between these forms of regulation. There are two reasons why this is done. First, pharmacy boards have the responsibility for the enforcement of both statutes and regulations; second, a statute regulation in effect in one state may appear as a pharmacy board regulation in another. New York, for example, has a statute prohibiting the advertising of prescription drug prices. The same prohibition appears as a pharmacy board regulation in Rhode Island. Both forms of regulation appear to have the same effect due to enforcement provisions which are vested in the state pharmacy boards.

There are twenty-five separate regulations specifically relating to the retail drug market in effect in the United States. Each of these regulations is in force in at least one state, and no state has all twenty-five. Six states are entirely unregulated. Regulations in the market have been grouped according to the aspects of the trade they concern. Table 2-1 lists the regulations and groupings. The Appendix describes each state in terms of the regulations in effect as of 1967.

1. *Ownership Prohibitions.* Explicit prohibition of pharmacy ownership is not a common type of regulation in the market. The only regulation of this form prohibits physicians from owning pharmacies due to the "conflict of interest" which exists when a physician writes prescriptions for, and sells prescriptions to, patients.

2. *Ownership Requirements.* Requirements for pharmacist ownership of retail pharmacies serve a dual purpose. First, they establish a ceiling on the number of firms in the market, second they serve to increase the homogeneity of the

Table 2-1

Regulations Enacted by State Legislatures and Boards of Pharmacy

1. *Ownership Prohibitions*
    1. Physician ownership of pharmacies prohibited
2. *Ownership Requirements*
    1. Pharmacist ownership of pharmacies required
3. *Merchandising Prohibitions*
    1. No pharmacy permit for a general merchandise store.
    2. No pharmacy permit for a "fair trade" violator.
4. *Limitations on Outlets*
    1. Limitation on the number of pharmacies in a state
5. *Physical Requirements*
    1. Physical separation required of prescription department in a general merchandise store
    2. Separate entrance mandatory for prescription department in a general merchandise store
    3. Entrance to adjoining store prohibited
    4. Floor space of prescription department of a minimum size
    5. Self-service for nonprescription products prohibited
    6. Minimum prescription inventory rule (as a percentage of total inventory)
    7. Ban on "closed door" operations
6. *Advertising Restrictions*
    1. Outdoor signs controlled
    2. Prohibition from implying discount prescription prices in advertising
    3. Advertising of prescription drug prices prohibited
    4. Promotional schemes (e.g., senior citizens discounts) prohibited
7. *Pharmacist Restrictions*
    1. Pharmacist manager requirement
    2. Pharmacist on duty whenever pharmacy is open
    3. Specification of hours a pharmacist works
    4. Specification of the number of pharmacists to be employed
    5. Specification of operating hours for pharmacy
    6. Prescription dispensing rules
8. *Regulation of Competing Distribution Methods*
    1. No prescription agents allowed
    2. Mail order drug sales prohibited
    3. Ban on sale of nonprescription drugs in vending machines

Source: Derived from F. Marion Fletcher, *Market Restraints in the Retail Drug Industry* (Philadelphia, Pennsylvania: University of Pennsylvania Press, 1967), pp. 272-273.

individuals supplying the market. This second feature has been found to be of particular importance in the maintenance of the competitive "status quo" in drug retailing.[14] Pharmacists as a group consider themselves to be health professionals rather than retail merchandisers. Only licensed pharmacists may dispense prescription drugs, thus pharmacists who have undergone similar training and share similar backgrounds tend to have a homogeneous view of their profession. The professional pharmacist stresses services provided rather than price as the criterion of performance.

3. *Merchandising Prohibitions*. Each regulation included under this classification has a different emphasis. The denial of a pharmacy permit to a general merchandise store denies existing variety, department, or chain organizations from including a pharmacy on the premises. Since pharmacies in such locations might be expected to generate a large sales volume at the expense of independent pharmacies, limiting their numbers will protect currently operating outlets.

In Mississippi, where fair trade laws are still in effect, the state pharmacy board has regulations which deny pharmacy permits to fair trade violators. (The regulation also provides for the revocation of permits for the same offense.) The regulation thus presents severe penalties for engaging in discounting practices.

4. *Limitation on Outlets*. At least one pharmacy board (Arkansas) is able to directly control the number of outlets in the state. The regulation enables boards to selectively grant pharmacy permits[15] and thus afford each pharmacy a protected market area.

5. *Physical Requirements*. Regulations affecting the physical structure of pharmacies are both numerous and varied. They have in common the regulation of relationships between prescription and nonprescription operations in the same outlet. Requirements for physical separation, separate entrance, prohibitions of entrance to adjoining stores may all serve to discourage large multi-product firms from expanding into the pharmacy business. While the same effects also hold true for the restriction of self-service, this regulation seems to specifically apply to discount type operations. The floor space and minimum inventory rules may effectively preclude large firms from the sector. These rules would require too large an area or too large a prescription inventory relative to the nonprescription operations. The ban on closed door operations would seem to preclude organizations which offer special discount prices to "members" from entering the market.

6. *Advertising Restrictions*. The regulations currently receiving the most attention from state legislators and consumer interest groups are related to restrictions on price advertising and other forms of promoting prescription drugs. Because they make price comparisons difficult or impossible, such regulations effectively limit the ability of pharmacies to compete on a price basis. In the absence of advertised prices the elimination of price competition may serve as a *de facto* means of maintaining higher than competitive price levels. These regulations also have a potential secondary effect of discouraging discounters and chains (which rely heavily on price advertising) from entering the market.

7. *Pharmacist Restrictions*. Employee regulations have the effect of providing employment to those in the pharmacy profession. They may have a derived effect of increasing the operating costs of pharmacies over what they might be in the absence of such regulation. The effect of this increase in wage expenses would be especially severe for the smallest firms.

8. *Regulation of Competing Distribution Methods*. Regulations enacted by pharmacy boards to limit sales by nonpharmacy outlets have the effect of staving off increased competition in the sale of nonprescription products and meeting competition developing in the sale of prescription drugs.

Bucklin notes that with the weakening of the fair trade laws, supermarkets and discount houses began to take on the most profitable nonprescription drug and cosmetic items previously available solely through drugstores.[16] Consumers were able to purchase these items, usually at lower prices, in alternative outlets in conjunction with food or other merchandise. This development has the effect of weakening the differentiation existing between drug and nondrug outlets. While currently these nonpharmacy outlets are not permitted to sell prescription drugs, entrance of multi-product variety outlets to the nonprescription drug market represents potential serious competition for smaller scale pharmacies.

A most interesting aspect of these regulations is they indicate that the power of pharmacy boards to regulate the retail distribution of prescription drugs is not limited to actual pharmacy operations, but extends to all methods used in the distribution of drugs.

**Public Policy Process in the
Retail Prescription Drug Market**

Figure 2-1 depicted the public policy process outcome, the "Retail Market Delivery System," as composed of two components: economic characteristics and the ability to provide for public health and safety. The relative emphasis society places on these two characteristics has apparently shifted toward the former. And while the latter should not, indeed cannot, be neglected as an area of interest and substance, the economic characteristics of the system are developed as our primary area of concern. Some evidence that this concern over the economic characteristics of the sector is not misplaced is supplied by a brief study of some current forces at work in the policy-making environment.

*The Issue of Current Forces: An
Illustration of Regulatory Assessment*[17]

The development of public policy is a response to the manifest needs and desires of the society. There is evidence that both the needs and desires of society relating to the production and distribution of drug products have evolved to a point where economic considerations have become at least as important as those of health and safety. The conditions which prompted initial regulation of the drug market are no longer apparent. Drug adulteration and the uncontrolled sale of dangerous drugs are no longer primary concerns of individuals. The conditions of product purity and efficacy are taken for granted as baseline assumptions by drug buyers. The ability of drug buyers to make such assumptions is undoubtedly related to the success of regulation in prohibiting unethical and unsafe practices through early drug production legislation.

As expenditures on drugs have increased, individuals and government agencies have begun to focus on the economic consequences of regulation. Public concern over these consequences represents the current force in the face of which policymakers are determining appropriate policy toward the retail drug sector. Current policy developments represent an examination of the potential trade-offs between benefits of health and safety and the economic consequences of regulation. In no area of retail regulation is assessment of this type more apparent than that of advertising regulation.

A discussion of the debate over the regulation of prescription drug price advertising sheds light on the evolving forces influencing regulatory activity. It also serves to point out the different conclusions reached concerning the effects of regulation as they relate to public health and safety and economic considerations.

As of 1967, twenty-nine states, by regulations or statutes, prohibited the advertisement of prescription drug prices. The issue of whether prescription drug price advertising should be regulated is the subject of current debate in most states where such regulations exist. Arguments for maintaining such regulations, and for their removal, revolve around the health and safety and economic consequences involved.

Advertising and the Objectives
of Health and Safety

Proponents of drug price advertising regulations have commonly cited the following arguments for prohibiting advertising with the objective of providing for public welfare:

1. Drug price advertising encourages patients to importune physicians to prescribe medication which may not be therapeutically necessary or that would be dangerous to their health.
2. It tends to encourage the prescribing and use of larger than needed quantities of drugs.
3. It tends to encourage patients to "shop around," thus making it difficult for pharmacists or physicians to monitor the drug usage of patients.
4. It would be contrary to the interests of the consumer and a possible threat to public health. There is most likely a relationship between illegal drug use and over-the-counter drug commercials. If advertising of prescription drugs is allowed, that can be added to the list of probable offenders.

Opponents of drug price advertising regulations are quick to discount these allegations. They assert that:

1. The prescribing physician has the ultimate control of both drugs and dosages of medication. No competent physician would submit to pressure to prescribe unneeded or dangerous medication.
2. Drugs would not be consumed in quantities larger than needed for proper treatment because: (a) physicians would have no reason to prescribe such quantities; (b) individuals would receive no physical benefit from taking drugs in quantities larger than those needed to control or cure an ailment or condition. To do so (take larger than needed quantities) would be to incur the cost of drugs with no concomitant benefit.
3. Where the patient receives all of his prescriptions from a single physician, the prescriber is still able to monitor drug usage patterns. In cases where individuals receive prescriptions from a number of physicians, the problem is neither aggravated nor reduced in the face of advertised prices. The issue of pharmacies monitoring patient drug usage is based on assumptions that: (a) individuals purchase all of their prescriptions from the same pharmacist, and, (b) that the dispensing pharmacists maintain records on drug buyers and advise them regarding appropriate usage. Even if these assumptions are true (and there is little evidence that they are) advertisement of prices does not preclude pharmacists from monitoring patient drug usage.
4. The asserted relationship between advertised drug prices and illegal drug use is fallacious. There is no evidence from which to conclude that advertising drug prices is causally linked to illicit drug use.

Advertising and Economic Issues

Economic considerations constitute the second focal point around which this debate revolves. Strong economic implications of deregulations are seen by both proponents and opponents of advertising restrictions. At issue is the interpretation of what implications would result from deregulation.

Proponents of advertising regulations assert:

1. Advertising will not lower prices of drugs because the cost of advertising will be passed on to the consumer.
2. Price posting will not necessarily reduce prescription prices, will reduce pharmacy services and will increase the likelihood of federal and injunctive activity for alleged price fixing.
3. Advertising will drive small independent pharmacists out of business because of the cost of advertising.
4. If advertising is permitted, "economic giants" and "opportunistic companies"

would seize the opportunity to achieve a "price cutter" or "discount" image by cutting prices. This will result in a price war which will drive out small pharmacies, after which the "giants," now in a monopoly situation, will raise prices to higher than current levels.

Opponents of drug price advertising regulations contend that the above arguments are basically in error:

1. There is some fractional evidence that suggests prescription prices are lower where advertising is permitted. In any event, even if prices are not lowered, the public has a basic right to know the price of a product at alternative outlets prior to actual sale.
2. There is no evidence to show that the amount of services provided or the quality of services decreases in areas where advertising is permitted. Where these services are desired by consumers, they can be profitably provided. The Justice Department has written an opinion that advertisement of prescription drug prices *per se* is not construed to be evidence of price fixing or collusion.
3. Where advertising is permitted there is no evidence of increased failure rate among small independents.
4. There is no evidence of a monopoly situation created. in localities where advertising is permitted.

In addition to these refutations, proponents of price advertising point out current "undesirable" conditions which advertising may help to alleviate.

1. Price variations for identical prescriptions are found among pharmacies in limited geographical areas. In the absence of price information consumers are not able to make informed decisions as to where they might prefer to purchase a prescription.
2. There is evidence of price discrimination on the part of some pharmacists. This discrimination can be linked to a lack of price information on the part of consumers.
3. Lack of price information is most costly to those who can least afford it—the elderly and the poor. These groups have a disproportionate incidence of illness which causes inordinate expenditures on drugs. The immobility associated with illness and poverty makes these individuals unable to physically shop around for low prescription prices.

Thus, there is ample evidence that the current forces with which policy-makers must contend have changed and are continuing to change. There is growing concern over the economic consequences of regulation. However, arguments proposed on both sides of the debate over drug price advertising (a single type of regulation) are based largely on assertion or a lack of supportive evidence. The actual economic consequences of regulation are not known.

The Effects of Regulation:
A Framework for Analysis

The primary purpose of analyzing the effects of implemented public policy is to provide a feedback mechanism for public policy decisionmakers, allowing an assessment of the effects of current policy and the development and implementation of new policy in a changing social environment.

A traditional analytic framework used in the study of markets is the industrial organization model. The basic elements of the model consist of structure, competitive conduct, and performance. Structure refers to the number and size distribution of sellers in the market, the relationships among sellers in the market, and the relations between existing firms and potential new entrants. Competitive conduct refers to the use of the assortment of variables which are under direct control of the firm. Conduct variables include price levels and price policies, product mix, promotional strategy, location, and so on. "The payoffs for the players, including society, in the competitive games in the marketing system is the performance of the system."[18] At the market level, prices, profits, and product assortment constitute primary indices of performance.

The industrial organization model assumes a relationship between structure, conduct, and performance such that market structure affects competitive conduct; conduct affects performance directly.

A primary criticism of this framework relates to oversimplification. The basic structure-conduct-performance model suggests that poor structure causes poor conduct which causes poor performance and feeds back to reinforce poor structure. Market structure has a direct influence on performance as well as an influence on performance through conduct. Perhaps more important, the model lacks the integration of environmental variables, which must be incorporated in order to understand differences in the effects of structural and conduct variables on performance.[19] Three other important criticisms have also been made of this model.[20] First, "the structure of the components of the system must concern not only firms, ... but also the physical establishments ..." Second, conduct feeds back not only to structure but also to the environment. Third, conduct variables need to be fully described on a market by market basis.[21]

In the analysis to follow these considerations are addressed explicitly. First, a major task of the study is to describe the environment of the retail drug market, most notably the regulatory environment, and to assess its impact on structure, conduct, and performance. Second, the analysis incorporates both firms and establishments. Third, the impact of competitive conduct on the market and the social environment is developed through the analysis of the performance of the market.

Monopolistic Competition and
the Retail Drug Market

Assume the market may be classified as monopolistically competitive, with the accompanying assumption that firms attempt to increase profits by varying price. This assumption requires that ". . . both demand and cost curves for all 'products' are uniform throughout the group [which requires] that consumers' preferences be evenly distributed among the different varieties, and that differences between them [the products] be not such as to give rise to differences in cost."[22]

Monopolistic Competition
and Free Entry

The short-run position of any firm in the market is shown in Figure 2-2. The differentiated nature of the market and an assumption of profit maximizing behavior leads any firm to move from an initial position of price, P_1, and output, Q_1, with profit, P_1ABC, by lowering price and increasing output. However, if it is profitable for one firm to lower price and increase output it will be profitable for all firms to make a similar move. All firms will attempt to maximize profits simultaneously, changes in price and quantity by one firm being matched by identical variation by competitors.

Each firm will not move along dd_1 as anticipated which assumes the output of the other $n-1$ firms constant, but instead moves along DD^1 which has a much steeper slope. Continuing to act in this manner in an attempt to increase profits, prices will be reduced and dd_1 moves downward along DD^1 until equilibrium point E where dd_1^1 is tangent to long-run average costs, profits are zero, price is P_2 and output Q_2.

Blockaded Entry

The result of the above analysis will occur, however, only under a condition of free entry to the market and an optimal number of firms at long-run equilibrium. If entry can be blockaded, firms will reap some, and possibly substantial, profits. Possible entry barriers in this market as previously noted are ownership requirements, specification of physical plant requirements and specification of operating procedures.

Free Entry and Restraints
on Price Competition

An alternative market condition offering results different from either of those presented above is that of free entry and a reliance on nonprice competition (Figure 2-3). This condition may arise from the regulation of prescription drug price advertising.

If price competition is lacking, due to tacit agreement or regulation of price advertising, individual firms will have no regard for the existence of curves such

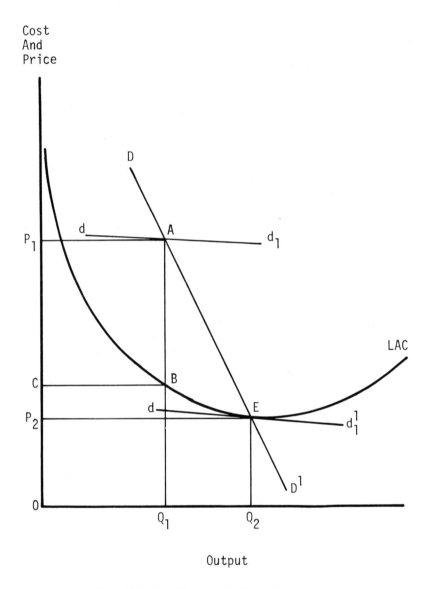

Figure 2-2. Equilibrium with Price Competition

as dd^1. Instead they will be concerned only with the effect of a general price rise or decline, i.e., DD_1.

With free entry in the absence of price competition, long-run equilibrium is attained only when enough firms have entered so that the individual firm's demand curve has shifted back to $D_1D_1^1$. Prices are at P_2 with output Q_2 and profits are zero. This equilibrium position leaves the market with many small

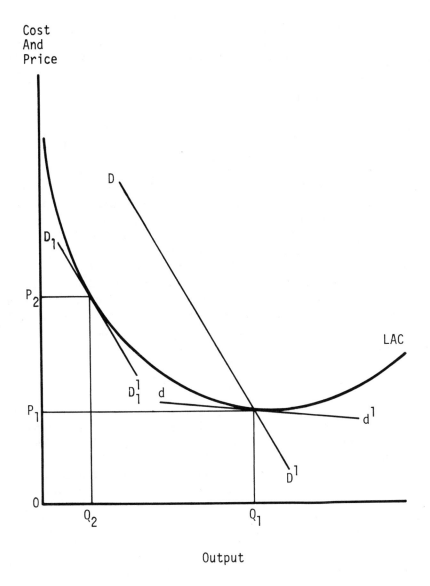

Figure 2-3. Equilibrium with Nonprice Competition

firms selling at prices substantially above minimal costs. The competition of new entrants has driven out profits but not market imperfections. Chamberlin concludes that a reliance on nonprice competition by firms

... protects, over short periods, their profits, but over long periods, their numbers, since when prices do not fall costs rise, the two being equated by the development of excess productive capacity. It may develop over long periods with impunity, prices always covering costs and may . . . become permanent and normal through a failure of price competition to function. The result is high prices and waste . . .[23]

Thus the observation of firms of varying efficiency in the market may be consistent with and indicative of a market exhibiting segments (states) which are differentially regulated; patterns of regulation ranging from completely unregulated to patterns affecting entry and price competition.

However, the observations of firms of diverse efficiency is not per se an indication of effectively regulated markets. The primary question regards the extent to which regulation, structure, conduct, and performance are related. As an alternative to regulatory impact firms and establishments of substantially different scale and output composition, services and prices may exist simultaneously due to the distribution of consumer demands and preferences. The imperfect distribution of consumers spatially in any market and inelastic demands for many products are primary elements in the development of monopolistic competition, and thus are also primary elements related to the development of optimal firm or establishment size as well as output composition. Markets with small widely spread populations or populations with low buying power cannot support large-scale multiproduct operations. Rather, scale of operation is small and likewise product variety is limited. Costs are resultantly high, profits limited. Where populations are larger, more dense, and have greater buying power, combinations of establishment structures may be seen coexisting. The population/income factor allows firms to achieve scale and output economies. At the same time, small specialized outlets may also exist by offering services, product assortment, and locational benefit to relatively small but profitable segments of the market.

Utilizing this framework of monopolistic competition it is possible to ascertain the market effects of regulation. This is done by examining the impact of the economic characteristics of the market which are associated with the development of market structure patterns and incorporating the regulations characterizing the market. That is, *given* the economic factors in the market, we will analyze the extent to which regulation affects market structure, competitive conduct and performance.

3 An Overview of the Market

The purpose of this chapter is to provide the reader with an overview of the retail prescription drug market. This section introduces the important variables of outlet classification, ownership patterns, product line composition, and expense patterns which are shown to be significant market characteristics when developed in greater detail in later chapters.

Structure

The supply structure of the retail prescription drug market refers to those retail outlets which sell prescription drugs to the public. Hospital pharmacies and public health programs which dispense drugs are thus excluded from consideration. Prescription drugs are those ingredients or combinations of ingredients designated by the Food and Drug Administration as being available on prescription (usually written by a physician or dentist). In addition to prescription drugs a majority of drugstores also sell nonprescription drugs referred to as "proprietary" or "over-the-counter" drugs, and a variety of general merchandise such as cosmetics, and other convenience products. Retail drug outlets are commonly classified on the basis of product variety offered and services provided. When classified in this manner, the outlets fall into one of five categories.[1]

Community Pharmacy. In terms of numbers of outlets, the community pharmacy segment dominates drug retailing. Community pharmacies sell prescription drugs, nonprescription drugs, health related products as well as a variety of general merchandise. These outlets are characterized by a limited trading area, low volume, and high markup. Typically, delivery, credit, and family prescription record services are provided.

Metropolitan Pharmacy. These outlets are located in central "downtown" locations. They are characterized by a high volume of general merchandise sales and frequently offer food service facilities. The volume of prescription sales is largely determined by the number of physicians practicing in the firm's trading area.

Discount Pharmacy. The discount pharmacies sell drug and health related products as well as a variety of general merchandise. They regularly offer a few allied services and are considered to be high volume, low margin merchandisers of prescription and nonprescription products.

Apothecary Pharmacy. These establishments sell only drugs and health related products. Apothecaries are usually located in or near a medical office building where a sufficient traffic in drugs enables them to remain economically viable.

Department Pharmacy. These pharmacies are operated as a separate section of a department store, and often are physically separate from the other sections of the store. These pharmacies are operated so that the products sold by the pharmacy do not compete with the merchandise sold in other sections of the store. The volume of prescription sales is dependent on the traffic generated by other areas of the store.

In 1967, there were 53,722 outlets classified as drugstores.[2] This figure represented a decrease of 1,010 units from the 1963 Census. A decline in the number of outlets in the sector has been a consistent pattern since 1939 when the number of establishments reached 58,000.[3]

The retail drug market has many characteristics commonly associated with small business. The majority of pharmacies have been and continue to be held in partnership or owned by sole proprietors. As might be expected given this ownership pattern, chain organizations are not as prevalent in the retail drug market as they are in other areas of retailing. Of the 46,244 establishments with payrolls in the sector, 39,621 are separate firms. These single establishment firms have much lower average sales than chains or small multiple establishment firms (Table 3-1).

An examination of the distribution to total sales across establishments classified according to size shows the pattern of change accompanying the decrease in number of outlets. Table 3-2 indicates that small outlets are losing market share to large units.[a]

Chain organizations have made consistent increases in sales and market share. In 1950 sales by chain pharmacies accounted for about 21 percent of retail pharmacy sales; in 1967 chain share of sales had increased to 33 percent. While total retail pharmacy sales increased 29 percent from $8.5 billion in 1963 to $11 billion in 1967, during the same period chains increased their total sales 70 percent. Chain organizations are making substantial increases in sales at the expense of independent single or multiple unit pharmacies.

Competition in the Market—
Product Lines

The pharmacy has evolved over time as a multiproduct retail institution. As Table 3-3 shows, in 1967, 71 percent of pharmacy sales consisted of drugs

[a]Alternatively, Table 3-2 portrays the growth of establishment sales over time, leaving relatively fewer firms in the lowest sales categories.

Table 3-1

Firms, Establishments, and Sales by Single and Multiple Unit Ownership*

Pharmacies	Firms	Establishments	Sales per Establishment
Total	39,621	46,244	$222,470
Single Units Total	38,000	38,000	$163,090
Operated by 1 establishment firms	37,766	37,766	161,810
Operated by multi-establishment firms	234	234	375,040
Multiple Units Total			
2 establishment multiple units	1,108	2,199	$200,930
3 establishment multiple units	236	703	261,560
4-5 establishment multiple units	127	531	304,970
6-10 establishment multiple units	71	486	446,390
11-25 establishment multiple units	36	543	647,350
26-50 establishment multiple units	19	662	712,430
51-100 establishment multiple units	14	872	832,500
101+ establishment multiple units	10	2,248	696,370

*Establishments refers to establishments in business for the entire year 1967.

Source: Derived from U.S., Department of Commerce, Bureau of the Census, *Census of Business*, 1967, I.

Table 3-2

Establishments by Volume: Percentage of Total Number of Establishments and Sales

	1958		1963		1967	
Annual Sales	Establishment	Sales	Establishment	Sales	Establishment	Sales
$1,000,000+	1%	16%	1%	10%	2%	17%
$500,000 - 999,999	2	—	3	13	6	19
$300,000 - 499,999	4	13	7	16	9	18
$100,000 - 299,999	37	47	45	46	43	36
Under $100,000	56	24	44	15	40	10
Total	100%	100%	100%	100%	100%	100%

Source: U.S., Department of Commerce, Bureau of the Census, *Census of Business, 1963, 1967*, I.

and proprietaries with the remainder of sales derived from various consumer products.

The pharmacy has come up against strong competition in many of these nonprescription drug product lines. The sale of nonprescription packaged medicine such as aspirin, and the sale of nonfood convenience products such as

Table 3-3

Distribution of Drugstore Sales Among Major Product Lines

	Sales	
Product Line	(000,000)	As a Percentage of Total Sales
Cosmetics–Drugs–Cleaners	$ 7,190	71%
Nonprescription medicines	[2,431]	[24]
Prescription medicine	[3,212]	[32]
All other drugs–proprietaries	[1,442]	[15]
Tobacco products	803	8
Alcoholic beverages	307	3
Meals, snacks	335	3
Groceries, other foods	208	2
Miscellaneous		
(Clothing, kitchenware, jewelry, appliances, etc.)	1,445	14
Total	$10,288	100%

Source: U.S., Department of Commerce, Bureau of the Census, *Census of Business, 1967*, I.

cosmetics in supermarkets represents one source of competition. The growth of large-scale general merchandise discount stores carrying packaged drugs and nondrug convenience merchandise represents still another. The impact of increased competition from these sources is shown in the changing composition of pharmacy sales.

Over the past twenty years prescription drugs have become the major revenue source for pharmacies. An examination of independent pharmacies finds a dramatic change in the growth of prescription drug sales as a percentage of total sales. In 1949, prescription drugs accounted for 19 percent of total independent drugstore sales. In 1971 prescription drugs accounted for 44.7 percent of sales for this group.[4] This change in the sales composition of independent retail pharmacies is due to the combination of two factors: increased competition in nonprescription product lines by pharmacy chains and nonpharmacy outlets; increased demand (from less than one billion dollars in 1949 to 4.5 billion in 1971) for prescription drugs.[b]

Performance–Costs and Profits

Independent pharmacies have also experienced decreased profits as a percentage of sales. Table 3-4 shows that in 1965 costs of goods sold was 63.8 percent of

[b]This is not to suggest that pharmacies have encountered no competition in the sale of prescription drugs. The development of new channels of distribution for prescription drugs such as public health service organizations and health maintenance organizations have served to reduce the monopoly power of the retail pharmacy as the source of prescription drugs.

Table 3-4

Cost of Goods Sold, Expenses, and Profits as a Percent of Sales—Independent Pharmacies, 1965-1971

Year	Sales	Cost of Goods Sold	Total Expenses	Profit
1965	100.0%	63.8%	30.4%	5.8%
1966	100.0	64.1	30.9	5.0
1967	100.0	64.1	31.1	4.8
1968	100.0	64.3	31.3	4.4
1969	100.0	63.8	31.7	4.5
1970	100.0	·63.9	32.0	4.1
1971	100.0	64.2	31.9	3.9

Source: Derived from *The Lilly Digest* (Indianapolis, Indiana: Eli Lilly and Company, 1972), p. 16.

sales, operating costs amount to 30.4 percent, and net profit reached a high of 5.8 percent. While cost of goods sold remained at about the same level in 1971 operating expenses for this group had risen to 31.9 percent resulting in a profit decline to 3.9 percent.

Chains have fared considerably better than the independents in maintaining profit levels. While the cost of goods sold remained stable for the period 1960-1970, operating costs decreased as a percentage of sales from 28.7 percent to 25.6 percent. Consequently, in 1970 chains showed a profit of 4.2 percent of sales, slightly greater than that of the independents.[5]

Summary

The taxonomy of retail drug outlets points to the diversity in the supply structure of the market, a structure characterized by single establishment firms. Over the past thirty-five years a consistent trend has been a decrease in the number of establishments in the market. While the average sales size of establishments has increased over the period the market is marked by the relative absence of the large firms found in other areas of retailing. Also notably absent are a large number of chain organizations. The growth in the sales size of establishments and the increasing market share of chain organizations suggests that there are economies of scale in pharmacy retailing. If this is the case a real question exists as to why large establishments and chain organizations did not develop in the market at an earlier time. A potential answer is that regulation, initiated primarily through the efforts of independent pharmacists, has effectively limited the entrance or growth of large-scale establishments and chains.

Cost functions and scale economies are examined in the following chapter. With the observation of a trend toward increased specialization in prescription drugs (especially among independent pharmacies) so apparent, the impact of establishment output between prescription and nonprescription products on costs is analyzed also.

4

Cost Functions and the Cost Structure of Pharmacy Retailing

This chapter examines the cost functions and the structure of costs in the retail drug market and serves several important purposes. The first of these is to determine the extent of economies of scale in the supply structure of the market. Second, the relationship between cost structure, establishment size, and output composition is examined. Third, cost related structural variables are identified for use in later analyses.

The first section of the chapter discusses some general problems of cost analysis and problems specific to the study of retail cost functions. Estimates of total and average cost functions are presented which show the cost effects of two major variables, establishment size and the composition of output. The structure of costs (fixed, discretionary and variable) for outlets is examined under varying conditions of establishment size and output composition.

Problems in Statistical Cost Analysis

Cost analysis in general and for retail markets in particular has associated problems which must be recognized in order to correctly qualify the derived results. These problems fall into four categories: measures of size, the estimation of costs, lack of homogeneity of firms or establishments, and the regression fallacy.[1]

Measures of Size. Scale of plant refers most commonly to units of homogeneous output. Where a firm or establishment is multiproduct, measures of output are ambiguous and size approximations must be based on other measures. At retail, where the majority of firms and establishments are multiproduct, the most common measures of size are sales volume, cost of goods sold, and number of transactions.[2] Estimates of size in terms of sales volume assume some standard bundle of services associated with each dollar sales and potentially confound output with conditions of demand or supply. Cost of goods sold as a measure of size provides a somewhat better estimate, eliminating markup policies among firms or outlets. In the estimates provided here measures of size are based primarily on dollar sales and cost of goods sold. It will be shown that these measures of output provide equivalent estimates. Because retail cost studies typically use sales-based size measures and for reasons of data comparability, the primary measure of size for this study is sales volume.

The Estimation of Costs. Cost estimation in general relies heavily on the use of accounting data. Such is the case in this study. The reliability of accounting data depends in turn on the method of allocation to cost components from some aggregate figure. In studies of retailing, a second problem arises due to the fact that a substantial portion of firm costs are "selling costs" which are incurred to change the position or slope of the demand curve. When some costs are incurred by a firm to change demand, then we must say that a part of the output of retailing is a change in demand.[3] This practice of incurring costs to change demand (differentiation) in an imperfect market creates an intermingling of costs and revenues, thus complicating sales-based size estimates.

Homogeneity of Firms. Closely related to problems of cost estimation are those of firm or established homogeneity. Interfirm and establishment cost comparisons implicitly "assumes that the (establishments) being compared are homogeneous with respect to output and productive factors."[4] This means that all firms having equal access to factors markets will select optimal inputs. Even the most casual observation of retailing is enough to discount any assumption of perfect homogeneity. The "marketing mix" of any class of retail establishments will differ (often substantially) with respect to product mix, allied services provided, and managerial expertise in selecting inputs. "The problem in empirical cost analysis is, therefore, to see that cross sectional data are from firms either with homogeneous output and factors or with identifiable differences in output and factor proportions."[5] As noted in the previous chapter output is not homogeneous among retail pharmacies. However, in our analysis it is possible to identify *differences* in output and to assess the impact of these differences on costs.

The Regression Fallacy. Friedman[6] and others[7] have developed elements of what is termed the "regression fallacy" in empirical cost analysis. This problem relates to differences in observed costs associated with differences between actual and anticipated demand.

Actual costs are incurred in anticipation of a given level of output. The relation of costs to planned output is not the same as their relation to unplanned output. Costs are likely to show some rigidity in the face of fluctuations in demand, particularly if the firm is seeking an average optimum cost over several short run periods. Unused capacity during periods of lower-than-planned sales and intensive use of capacity during periods of greater-than-planned sales will result in actual cost, revenue relationships different from those which would have occurred had planned outputs and planned costs been experienced.[8]

This problem is especially relevant to cost studies of retail markets where fixed and discretionary costs make up the bulk of total outlet costs. These are incurred in anticipation of some level of demand and are not subject to sudden changes. Johnston's studies in statistical cost analysis lead him to conclude that the effects of the regression fallacy are not likely to seriously bias results.[9] Where firms are grouped on the basis of size classification as in this study the effects of unused capacity and intensively used capacity appear to be offsetting.

The remainder of this chapter develops:

1. Total and average cost functions for retail pharmacies.
2. The impact of prescription drug and nonprescription output on cost functions.
3. The impact of establishment size on the level and structure of costs.
4. The impact of output composition on the level and structure of costs.

The Data

The data used in the development of this cost analysis are derived from a sample of 3,183 independent and chain-owned pharmacies. The data were collected by Eli Lilly and Company in 1970 as part of a continuous survey of retail pharmacy operations. Comparable data are collected annually.[10]

This sample was divided into seventy-one mutually exclusive groupings of establishments by total sales size and prescription drug volume. The data from each respondent in each grouping is averaged with those from respondents in the same size grouping. The result of this processing is seventy-one observations of an average or "typical" pharmacy of given sales and prescription volume.

Empirical Results: Total Costs

The total cost function was estimated utilizing total operating expenses as the dependent variable. The function was estimated using alternatively total sales and cost of goods sold as independent variables. Although both equations yield comparable estimates of total costs, Table 4-1 shows that the total sales equation yields slightly better results in terms of explained variance. Because of this and the fact that dollar sales are the most commonly used output measure in retail costs studies, the discussion to follow refers to "sales" when the term "output" is used. Throughout this chapter all sales figures are in thousands of dollars.

As shown by the scatter diagram in Figure 4-1, the relationship between total cost and sales appears to be linear. This appraisal is confirmed when squared and cubic terms are added to the equation adding little in explanatory power.

Average Costs

Our primary interest is with average costs and the existence of economies of scale. A linear total cost function implies a specific shape for the average cost

Table 4-1
Estimates of Total Cost

Equation	Total Cost		a		Total Sales	Cost of Goods Sold	R^2
1	Y	=	28574	+	191.56 (56.2)		.989
2	Y	=	34090			+ 257.52 (50.2)	.986

( ) = "t" value
$n = 71$

curve. Specifically, marginal and average variable costs will be equal and constant; average fixed costs approach marginal costs and remain constant over large range of output. Where the intercept is positive, average variable costs will initially be above marginal costs and rapidly approach marginal cost as output increases. Furthermore, this function connotes no diseconomies at high levels of output.[11]

The transformation suggested by the linear total cost function for estimating average costs

$$AC = a + b\,(1/X),$$

where:

$$X = \text{total sales},$$

yields the estimate,

$$AC = 260.68 + 8067.07\,(1/X) \qquad (4.1)$$
$$(7.4)$$

$$R^2 = .443$$

This relationship is shown in the scatter diagram in Figure 4-2 and conforms to the anticipated function. No diseconomies are witnessed over the output range considered.

Economies of scale are substantial. The smallest (primarily independent) pharmacies with less than $100,000 sales volume exhibit average costs up to 36 percent of sales. Compared to these, establishments in the over $2,500,000 range have average costs of around 19 percent of sales, or almost half the level of the smaller pharmacies. Scale economies up to approximately one million dollars in sales volume are significant, with economies decreasing but still in evidence for sales up to three million dollars.

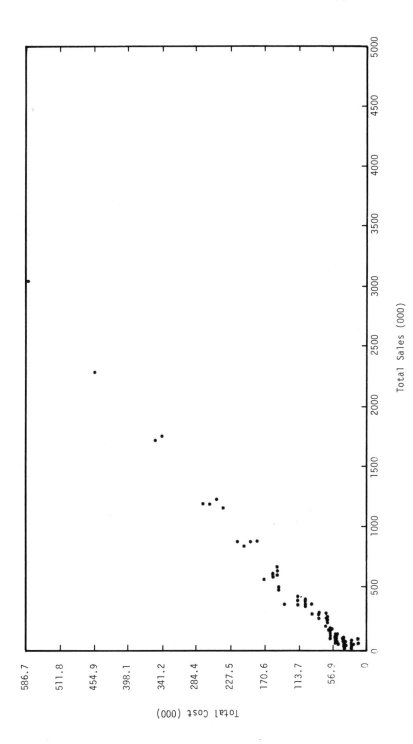

Figure 4-1. Relationship Between Total Cost and Total Sales

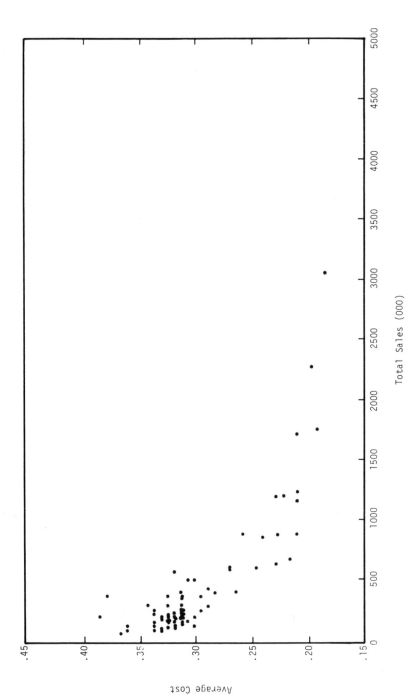

Figure 4-2. Relationship Between Average Cost and Total Sales

The Impact of Output Composition

One of the assumptions underlying this cost analysis is that differences in output composition among establishments do not give rise to differences in costs. An examination of the plot of average costs, however, shows that at several levels of output establishments exhibiting differing average costs are observed. A closer look at these observations is enlightening, for in all cases where different average costs are observed for establishments with similar volumes of total sales, average costs vary directly with the proportion of output consisting of prescription sales. Selected examples of this finding for independent pharmacies are shown in Table 4-2.

Average costs appear to be significantly related not only to the level of total output, but to the composition of total output between prescription and nonprescription sales.

This relationship may be estimated as

$$AC = a + b(1/X_1) + cX_2$$

where:

X_1 = Total Sales

X_2 = Prescription sales/total sales

$$AC = 240.89 + 4719.48(1/X_1) + 93.84(X_2) \tag{4.2}$$
$$(3.42) \qquad (3.63)$$

$$R^2 = .53$$

For any level of total sales, average costs increase with the proportion of total output accounted for by prescription drug sales.[a] It is not sufficient to estimate average costs as a function of X_2 alone due to the fact that smaller outlets tend to have a higher proportion of output consisting of prescription drugs. An estimate of average cost as a function of X_2 would confound the characteristics of size and output composition.

The Structure of Costs

From the nature of the average cost function, it is obvious that significant scale economies exist over the output range considered. It is useful to examine the

---

[a]It should be noted that increases in sales of prescription drugs are not associated with increases in average costs per se. Increases in average costs will be incurred only when there is no simultaneous increase in nonprescription sales as well, resulting in a higher proportion of total output consisting of prescription products.

Table 4-2

Total Output, Proportion of Output in Prescription Drug Sales, and Average Costs

Observation	Total Sales	Prescription Sales Total Sales	Average Costs (% of sales)
1	$ 85,296	46.7	33.3
2	85,751	75.0	36.1
3	109,411	31.1	30.6
4	109,841	47.8	32.2
5	110,471	55.6	32.3
6	109,394	77.1	33.7
7	273,914	22.7	28.9
8	269,716	36.6	31.6
9	271,275	47.6	32.4
10	273,703	62.1	34.3

structure of costs in order to determine how the components of cost are affected by output levels and the composition of output. While by definition all costs are variable in the long run, in order to facilitate the discussion classifications of fixed, discretionary and variable are used as nominal groupings.

Fixed Costs

Fixed costs considered here correspond to the traditional definition of being invariate, in the short run, with changes in output. The long-run average cost curve reported above infers that some costs are fixed in the long run also. Included in this category are rent, interest payments, insurance, and taxes.

Discretionary Costs

Discretionary costs, like fixed costs, do not vary with output in the very short run. They may or may not exist at the zero output level and may be altered over a short-run planning period, i.e., they may be reassessed annually.

"Discretionary costs, in short, are costs which are fixed with respect to output variation but are decision variables within the functional time period known as the short run."[1,2]

In this category are included utilities expenses, service fees, repairs, telephone, advertising, proprietor's or manager's salary. Also included are employees' wages. Wage costs are traditionally treated as variable costs. However, Holdren has shown that innovation in food retailing involved a shifting of wages from variable to discretionary costs due to an increased specialization of labor. This argument can be made especially relevant in the retail prescription drug market. In order to dispense any prescription drugs, a pharmacist must be employed. For small outlets, the owner-manager usually fulfills this function of drug dispensing and performs other clerical and clerking duties as well. However, unless he is able to perform all functions, some wage expenses must be incurred regardless of output. In larger outlets, which may be open eighty or more hours per week, several pharmacists must be employed. In many states a pharmacist must be on duty whenever the pharmacy is open regardless of whether or not any prescription drugs are sold. Additionally, in larger outlets, clerks would tend to be unionized and management would hire employees to meet periods of normal demand resulting in underutilization of labor in slack periods and full utilization (and division of labor between prescription and nonprescription selling) in periods of peak demand. Labor allocation decisions will thus be made on projected output forecasts and are essentially discretionary in nature.

Variable Costs

The bulk of operating costs fall into one of the above categories. Purely variable costs consist of delivery and bad debts charged off.

**Average Cost Components, Output
and Output Composition**

Table 4-3 shows how average fixed, average discretionary, and average variable costs vary by outlet size. Table 4-4 shows how these costs vary with respect to the composition of output (i.e., by prescription volume as a proportion of total sales). Consistent with the discussion above, the components of average cost decrease as outlet size increases, and increase as the proportion of prescription sales increase.

Table 4-5 provides estimates of the components of average cost as a function of total establishment sales size and output composition.

Fixed Costs

The estimates of average fixed costs

$$AFC = 51.1 + 1924.65X_1 - 1.56X_2 \qquad (4.3)$$
$$(5.4) \qquad (.05)$$

$$R^2 = .43$$

Table 4-3
Independent Pharmacy Operating Costs as a Percentage of Sales, by Sales Size

Item		Sales Size Category			
	−$100,000	$100,000-200,000	$200,000-300,000	$300,000-400,000	$400,000+
Fixed Costs	7.44	6.28	6.08	5.70	5.80
Rent	3.48	2.60	2.40	2.30	2.40
Taxes	1.20	1.30	1.36	1.40	1.40
Insurance	.82	.80	.80	.80	.80
Interest	.72	.50	.46	.30	.30
Depreciation	1.22	1.08	1.06	.90	.90
Discretionary Fixed	26.12	25.22	25.25	25.40	25.20
Salary	14.00	10.10	8.13	6.90	5.60
Wages	6.74	9.92	12.00	13.50	14.30
Utilities	.84	.80	.73	.70	.70
Services	.44	.36	.40	.40	.30
Repairs	.34	.34	.33	.30	.30
Advertising	1.18	1.32	1.36	1.40	1.50
Telephone	.56	.36	.30	.30	.20
Miscellaneous	2.02	2.02	2.00	1.90	2.30
Variable Costs	.90	.68	.63	.60	.50
Delivery	.70	.50	.43	.40	.30
Bad Debts	.20	.18	.20	.20	.20
Total Average Costs	34.46	32.18	31.96	31.70	31.50

Table 4-4

Independent Pharmacy Operating Costs as a Percentage of Sales, by Proportion of Prescription Drug Sales

Item	Proportion of Prescription Sales				
	15-30%	31-45%	46-60%	60-75%	75% +
Fixed Costs	6.00	5.93	5.77	6.00	7.50
Rent	2.56	2.30	2.17	2.60	4.10
Taxes	1.30	1.40	1.37	1.20	1.30
Insurance	.77	.80	.80	.80	.80
Interest	.40	.43	.40	.40	.40
Depreciation	.97	1.00	1.03	1.00	.90
Discretionary Fixed	22.87	25.17	26.17	26.80	28.70
Salary	5.96	7.53	8.83	9.80	12.00
Wages	12.00	12.37	12.00	11.80	11.40
Utilities	.87	.80	.77	.70	.40
Services	.37	.37	.40	.40	.50
Repairs	.37	.33	.37	.30	.20
Advertising	1.30	1.40	1.43	1.40	.90
Telephone	.20	.27	.37	.40	.50
Miscellaneous	1.80	2.10	2.00	2.00	2.80
Variable Costs	.37	.54	.70	.80	1.10
Delivery	.27	.37	.50	.60	.80
Bad Debts	.10	.17	.20	.20	.30
Total Average Costs	29.24	31.64	32.64	33.60	37.30

Table 4-5

Relationship Between Average Components of Operating Expense, Total Sales, and Output Composition

Expense Item as a Proportion of Total Expenses	Intercept	X_1 (1/total sales)	X_2 (prescription sales/ total sales)	R^2
Rent	.115	−.068 (.00)	+.047 (2.20)	.14
Taxes	.047	+.023 (.00)	−.147 (2.0)	.09
Insurance	.015	+.377 (1.2)	+.009 (1.7)	.21
Interest	.004	+1.33 (5.62)	+.002 (.05)	.50
Depreciation	.029	+1.20 (4.52)	−.011 (2.25)	.25
Average Fixed Costs	51.16	+1924.65 (5.40)	−1.56 (.05)	.43
Salaries	.084	+17.26 (11.21)	+.175 (6.03)	.87
Wages	.438	−17.99 (13.90)	+.005 (.20)	.84
Utilities	.032	+1.34 (9.8)	−.033 (12.82)	.71
Services	.004	+.313 (1.85)	+.010 (3.28)	.37
Repairs	.014	+.088 (.75)	−.009 (4.72)	.33
Advertising	.065	−1.71 (2.86)	−.019 (1.63)	.32
Telephone	.002	+.563 (6.8)	+.010 (6.53)	.81
Miscellaneous	.151	−3.18 (2.18)	−.110 (4.0)	.47
Average Discretionary Costs	190.31	+2613.32 (2.5)	+84.17 (4.1)	.50
Delivery	−.001	+.457 (3.62)	+.025 (10.62)	.83
Bad Debts	.001	+.001 (.00)	+.008 (5.1)	.41
Average Variable Costs	−.582	+182.23 (2.45)	+11.22 (4.16)	.82

where:

AFC = Average fixed costs

X_1 = 1/total sales

X_2 = Prescription sales/total sales

shows decreasing average fixed costs associated with increases in total sales volume, but that output composition has no effect on these costs ($t < 1.0$). From estimate (4.4) and (4.5), it is clear that the largest outlets[b] have significantly higher sales per square foot of outlet area, which suggests that the capital/output ratio decreases as outlet size increases.

$$Y_1 = .1867 + .00003X \qquad (4.4)$$
$$(2.37)$$
$$R^2 = .110$$

$$Y_2 = .0186 + .00002X \qquad (4.5)$$
$$(8.3)$$
$$R^2 = .605$$

where:

Y_1 = Prescription sales per square foot

Y_2 = Nonprescription sales per square foot

X = Total outlet size (square feet)

Discretionary Costs

Average discretionary costs are significantly related in sales volume increases and by increases in the proportion of output composed of prescription drugs.

$$ADFC = 190.31 + 2613.32X_1 + 84.17X_2 \qquad (4.6)$$
$$(2.5) \qquad (4.1)$$
$$R^2 = .50$$

where:

$ADFC$ = Average discretionary costs

X_1 = 1/total sales

X_2 = Prescription sales/total sales

The two largest components of discretionary costs, salary and wages, display an interesting pattern (Table 4-5). Managers' salaries decrease as a percentage of sales as total sales increase, but as the proportion of output accounted for by prescription drugs increases, so do salaries. In the former case, as total sales increase (and holding the proportion of prescription sales constant) additional labor must be added as clerks and other hourly employees. For higher

[b]Largest in terms of physical size. The simple correlation between physical size in square feet and total sales volume is .858. Relationship is for independent pharmacies only.

proportion prescription drug outlets, the opposite effect occurs. For any given level of sales, the higher the proportion of prescription drugs sold, the fewer clerks needed to care for nonprescription customers. The owner-manager is able to perform a greater amount of total selling activity. The differential in pay between the pharmacist and clerk tends to reflect itself in higher average labor expenses for the more specialized pharmacy.

Variable Costs

Variable costs display an expected pattern. As the proportion of prescription drugs increases, delivery expenses (delivery to customers) increase. These prescription specialists typically offer such auxiliary services as a means of attracting sales. It is not so clear, however, why bad debts should be related to a higher proportion of prescription sales. A probable answer is that credit services are offered by these firms to a greater extent than outlets which are less prescription oriented.

$$AVC = -.582 + 182.23X_1 + 11.22X_2 \qquad (4.7)$$
$$(2.45) \qquad (4.16)$$

$$R^2 = .82$$

where:

AVC = Average variable cost

X_1 = 1/total sales

X_2 = Prescription sales/total sales

Summary of Cost and Structure

Significant economies of scale exist over wide ranges of output in the retail prescription drug market. Average costs decrease rapidly for increases in total sales up to approximately one million dollars and at a decreasing rate thereafter. These economies are promoted primarily by the more efficient use of capital by larger establishments and their more productive and specialized use of labor. Sales size of establishment is a major structural variable in the market.

The composition of output between prescription and nonprescription sales, as well as the absolute level of each, significantly affects average costs. Increases in the proportion of sales accounted for by prescription drugs at any level of total output are associated with higher costs. These higher costs are attributable to higher labor costs, higher capital costs, and the provision of services associated with prescription drug sales, such as delivery and credit. The majority of establishments in this sample operate at substantially lower than the million dollar sales volume level. Average sales for the group are only slightly over $450,000.

This chapter concludes the general discussion of the structure of the retail prescription drug market. From here our attention will be focused on the impact of regulation on market structure and the effects of regulatory impact. In Chapter 5 we will examine the distribution of establishment size in the market. Also undertaken is an analysis of the effect of regulation on the composition of output and the form under which establishments are organized.

5

Structural Effects and Structural Costs of Regulation

In the previous two chapters the structure of the retail prescription drug market and the long-run average cost function of establishments in the market were examined. In this and succeeding chapters the effects of regulation in this market are examined.

This chapter analyzes the effects of regulation on market structure. The specific purposes of this analysis are to estimate the impact of regulation on market structure and to derive the costs borne by society resulting from regulatory impact on structure. These purposes are met through an examination of the relationship between regulation and average establishment sales size, output composition, establishment sales size distribution, and the organizational form of establishments in the market.

The Data

The data used in this cross-sectional state analysis are drawn from the 1967 *Census of Business-Retail Trade Reports; The Statistical Abstract*, 1969 and the market regulations presented in Chapter 2. The state of Hawaii is excluded from the analysis due to insufficient data, the District of Columbia is included; the calculations presented in this chapter are thus based on fifty observations. These data are grouped into three categories:

1. Structural Market Characteristics
2. Economic Market Characteristics
3. Regulatory Market Characteristics.

Structural Market Characteristics

Structural market characteristics are the following:

ESTAB   The number of pharmacies with payroll in a state.

SALES   Total sales of all pharmacies in a state (000).

AVESALES   Average dollar sales of all pharmacies in a state (000).

CHAIN11   Proportion of pharmacies in a state belonging to a chain of 11 or more establishments.

CHAIN4   Proportion of pharmacies in a state belonging to a chain of 4 or more establishments.

3HUNDRED   Proportion of pharmacies in a state having sales of \$300,000 or more.

5HUNDRED   Proportion of pharmacies in a state having sales of \$500,000 or more.

MILLION   Proportion of pharmacies in a state having sales of \$1,000,000 or more.

PROPOR   The proportion of total sales accounted for by prescription drugs.

Economic Market Characteristics

POP   State population (000).

DENSITY   State population per square mile (000).

PCPI   State per capita personal income.

Regulatory Market Characteristics[a]

Regulations affecting the market presented in Chapter 2 were grouped into eight categories:

R_1 Ownership Prohibitions

R_2 Ownership Requirements

R_3 Merchandising Prohibitions

R_4 Limitation on Outlets

R_5 Physical Requirements for Outlets

R_6 Advertising Restrictions

R_7 Pharmacist Restrictions

R_8 Regulation of Competing Distribution Methods

     Each regulatory category contains from one to seven regulations of similar emphasis:

---

[a]There is little evidence to suggest that either *Ownership Prohibitions* (restricting only physicians from owning pharmacies, or *Pharmacist Restrictions* (dealing with the utilization of pharmacist labor) would have an impact on the market structure variables considered in this section. Therefore, in order to reduce the number of independent variables, *Ownership Prohibitions* and *Pharmacist Restrictions* are excluded from the estimates to be presented. Estimates which included these variables revealed them to be insignificant in all cases.

Category	Regulations Included
R_1	Physician Ownership of pharmacies prohibited.
R_2	Pharmacist ownership required.
R_3	No pharmacy permit for a general merchandise store. No pharmacy permit for a Fair Trade violator.
R_4	Limitations on the number of pharmacies in a state.
R_5	Physical separation required of prescription department in general merchandise store. Separate entrance mandatory for prescription department in a general merchandise store. Entrance to adjoining store prohibited. Floor space of prescription department of minimum size (as a percentage of total floor space or over 220 square feet). Self-service prohibited for proprietary products. Minimum prescription inventory rule (as a percentage of total inventory). Ban on closed door operations.
R_6	Outdoor signs controlled. Prohibition from implying discount prescription prices in advertising. Advertising of prescription drug prices prohibited. Promotional schemes prohibited.
R_7	Pharmacist-manager requirement. Pharmacist on duty whenever pharmacy is open. Specification of number of pharmacists to be employed. Specification of operating hours for pharmacy. Specification of hours a pharmacist works. Prescription dispensing rules.
R_8	No prescription agents allowed. Mail order drug sales prohibited. Ban on sale of proprietary drugs in vending machines.

Each state was examined for the presence of regulations. The eight regulatory categories were treated as dummy variables. If a state had any regulation contained in a category, the state received a "1" for that category and a "0" otherwise. This process continued until each state was classified according to its pattern of regulation.[b]

Estimation

The general model used to estimate the effects of regulation and economic characteristics on market structure is:

$$Y = a + b_1 X_1 + \ldots + b_m X_m + c_1 Z_1 + \ldots + c_m Z_m$$

where:

Y is a market structure variable

$X_1 \ldots X_n$ are economic characteristics of the market

$Z_1 \ldots Z_m$ are regulatory characteristics of the market

Our initial interest centers on the examination of two variables: the average sales size of establishments and the composition of establishment sales between prescription and nonprescription products. As developed in Chapter 4, both sales size of establishments and output composition are related to long-run average costs; regulatory impact on these variables will resultantly impact on costs.

Average Sales Size and Regulation

Average sales per establishment were estimated as a function of per capita income, population density, and the regulatory dummy variables. The economic "dollar and distance" variables are hypothesized to be positively related to average sales per establishment; the regulatory variables are hypothesized to be negatively related.

$$\text{AVESALES} = f(\text{PCPI}, \text{DENSITY}, R_2, R_3, R_4, R_5, R_6, R_8) \qquad (5.1)$$

---

[b]An alternative way to examine the structural effects of regulation would be to consider the number of regulations in each category and attempt to measure any cumulative effects of regulation. Estimates using this procedure proved to be generally inferior in explaining variance and identifying significant relationships among variables to those presented here.

$$\text{AVESALES} = 49.9 + .0067\text{PCPI} + .0170\text{DENSITY} - 29.82R_2$$
$$\qquad\qquad (2.61) \qquad (2.59) \qquad\qquad (.71)$$

$$- 25.63R_3 - 36.47R_4 - 8.16R_5 - 60.45R_6 + 39.36R_8$$
$$\quad (.51) \qquad (.09) \qquad (.37) \qquad (2.09) \qquad (1.33)$$

$R^2 = .419$

Both higher income and higher population density, representing market potential, are significantly related to increase in average sales. All of the regulations except R_8, *Regulation of Competing Distribution Methods*, have the expected negative sign. The positive coefficient of R_8, while not significant at the .10 level, indicates perhaps that in states where competing methods of distribution (such as vending machines or mail order drug firms) are prohibited, current market members are able to increase average sales due to a decrease in the amount of intertype competition. This indication is examined in greater detail later in this chapter.

Only one regulatory variable, R_6, *Advertising Restrictions*, has a significant effect on establishment average sales size. The coefficient indicates that in states regulating prescription drug advertising, average sales per establishment in 1967 were $60,000 lower than in regulated states. With average sales size of establishments in the market approximately $248,000 in that year, the lower sales level in regulated states is significant by any criterion. In turn, with the presence of scale economies, average costs will be higher for establishments in states where price advertising is prohibited. The ability of firms to advertise prices permits (but does not guarantee) active price competition in the market. With price information provided to potential buyers, managers will view firm demand curves as highly elastic, expecting to gain customers from other firms by decreasing prices and to lose customers from price increases. This situation corresponds perfectly to the "active price competition" case described in Chapter 2. Average firm size increases and differences between price and long-run costs are minimal. Similarly, fewer firms may be present in the price informed markets because very small scale, high cost firms may be at a serious competitive disadvantage.

To test this proposition, the number of establishments in each state was estimated as a function of per capita income, population density and a dummy variable representing *Advertising Restrictions*.

$$\text{ESTAB} = f'\,(\text{PCPI}, \text{DENSITY}, R_6) \qquad\qquad\qquad (5.2)$$
$$\text{ESTAB} = -969.5 + .484\text{PCPI} - .0063\text{DENSITY} + 410.99R_6$$
$$\qquad\qquad (2.42) \qquad (1.13) \qquad\qquad (2.04)$$

$R^2 = .238$

The negative coefficient of DENSITY, while insignificant at the .10 level, suggests that greater population density is associated with fewer establishments. As seen in (5.1), DENSITY has a significantly positive relationship with average sales size of establishments, thus the negative coefficient appears to be in the appropriate direction, indicating larger but fewer establishments in states with relatively high population density.

Both per capita income and the presence of advertising restrictions are positively related to the number of pharmacies operating in a state. Taken together with (5.1) the estimate suggests that the regulation of advertising is positively associated with a significantly larger number of smaller pharmacies.[c]

Output Composition and Regulation

The second aspect of costs potentially affected by regulation is output composition. For the pharmacy, as developed in Chapter 4, increases in the proportion of total sales consisting of prescription drugs is related to increases in average cost. (R_7, *Pharmacist Restrictions*, is included in this estimate to determine the relationship between degree of specialization in prescription drugs and requirements for pharmacist utilization.)

$$\text{PROPOR} = g(\text{AVESALES}, \text{DENSITY}, R_2, R_3, R_4, R_5, R_6, R_7, R_8) \quad (5.3)$$

$$\text{PROPOR} = 43.18 - .0556\text{AVESALES} - .0003\text{DENSITY}$$
$$\qquad\qquad\quad (2.25) \qquad\qquad (.25)$$

$$- 8.99R_2 - .1881R_3 + 7.40R_4 + 7.08R_5$$
$$(1.41) \quad (.01) \qquad (.60) \qquad (1.93)$$

$$+ 7.75R_6 - 3.53R_7 - 4.11R_8$$
$$(1.28) \qquad (.87) \qquad (.85)$$

$R^2 = .285$

---

[c]The standard error of the *Advertising Restrictions* coefficient is quite large indicating a certain amount of noise in the estimate. Ninety-five percent confidence limit values of the coefficient are 5.2 and 916.8. Thus, while the absolute "numbers" effect of the restriction of advertising on the number of pharmacies is somewhat difficult to estimate, the "significant" effect, i.e., an association with larger numbers of smaller pharmacies, is quite clear.

It is possible that the significance of the coefficient is a proxy for other regulations affecting the number of establishments. An estimate which included all other regulatory variables, population and per capita income indicated that *Advertising Restrictions* is the only regulatory variable whose coefficient exceeded the standard error ($b = 66.3, t = 1.42$). While the "t" value of *Advertising Restrictions* in this estimate is not as great as in (5.2) the magnitude of the coefficient appears reasonable.

Consistent with relationships developed earlier a higher proportion of prescription drug sales is a characteristic of smaller outlets. Economic market characteristics such as population density have no effect on output composition. The only regulatory variable affecting PROPOR is R_5, *Physical Requirements for Outlets*. These requirements, as hypothesized in Chapter 2, have the effect of making the entry of development of large-scale merchandise firms difficult, due to restrictions on the allocation of floor space, inventories, and the physical accessibility of the prescription department. On average, states regulating the physical characteristics of outlets between prescription and nonprescription departments have establishments with a 7 percent higher ratio of prescription sales to total sales than unregulated states.

Estimates of the Structural Costs of Regulation

As shown above, regulation of advertising and regulation of the physical characteristics of outlets are associated with firms with smaller sales volume than firms in unregulated markets. This leads to a waste of resources because regulation allows drug retailers to operate at less than the most efficient scale given the economic characteristics of the market in which they are located. The opportunity cost of these wasted resources will be referred to as structural costs. The term structural cost is used because costs may also accrue to drug purchasers in the form of price effects of regulation. These price effects will be analyzed in later sections of the study.

An estimate of the magnitude of structural costs may be made by considering the average sales level and output composition of the thirty-five states in which regulation of advertising or physical characteristics or both types of regulation are found compared to what these sales and output composition values would be if these states were unregulated. These differences in sales volume and output composition may then be translated into costs by substituting into the long-run average cost estimates developed in Chapter 4. Consider:

$$AC = 240.88 + 4719.48X_1 + 98.34X_2$$

where:

X_1 = 1/total sales (000)

X_2 = Prescription sales/total sales (000)

as the average cost function for any establishment in the market.

Since average costs are derived as a percentage of sales, an estimate of the structural costs of regulation may be estimated by substituting the values of the variables AVESALES and PROPOR into the equation for all states having regulations R_5, R_6 or both and multiplying by total sales for those states. This total cost figure is compared to one derived from substituting the values AVESALES and PROPOR estimated from (5.1) and (5.3), that is, the values for AVESALES and PROPOR if the states were unregulated. The difference in these two estimates is the cost of misallocation borne by society and attributable to regulation.

Conceptually, these costs may be broken down into two categories: excessive costs of output produced, and value (above cost) of output foregone.

In Figure 5-1, $C_1 A Q_1 O$ represents the cost of producing output Q_1 (output under regulation). $C_2 B Q_1 O$ represents the cost of producing output Q_1 in the absence of regulation.

The cost of regulation (TC_R) for this output is computed as

$$TC_R = (Q_1 C_1 - Q_1 C_2)$$

A second cost component is associated with the differences in output $(Q_2 - Q_1)$ attributable to regulation. Where regulation exists affecting pharmacy sales size output is restricted by the amount $(Q_2 - Q_1)$. By assumption, the larger sales by pharmacies in unregulated states cannot represent prescription drug sales.[d] Thus the greater output of pharmacies in unregulated states must take the form of sales of some complementary nonprescription products. This additional output of nonprescription products in unregulated states may represent one of two conditions: a general increase in demand for nonprescription products sold by pharmacies; a shift in outlet preference by consumers for nonprescription products from, say, supermarkets or proprietary drugstores.

If $(Q_2 - Q_1)$ represents only a shift in consumer preference for purchasing nonprescription products to pharmacies and away from some other type of retail outlet then the cost of regulation remains as calculated above.[e]

However, if $(Q_2 - Q_1)$ represents a general increase in the demand for pharmacy products then the amount 1/2 ABCD (from Figure 5-1) must be added to the costs of regulation and they are calculated as

$$TC_R = Q_1 (C_1 - C_2) + \tfrac{1}{2} [(Q_2 - Q_1)(C_1 - C_2)]$$

---

[d]The demand for prescription drugs is basically a function of the health "index" of a community given some demographic characteristics. Physicians write prescriptions; the choice for individuals with a prescription is (a) whether or not to purchase the prescription and (b) at which pharmacy to fill the prescription. See Chapter 8 for further examination of this issue.

[e]No costs are incurred for $(Q_2 - Q_1)$ (output foregone) because this output has not been changed, but merely been reapportioned among retailers selling products also offered by pharmacies.

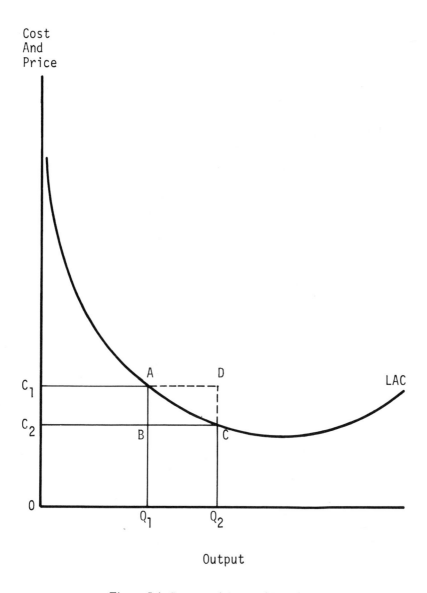

Figure 5-1. Structural Costs of Regulation

The above distinction allows a computation of a "high" and "low" estimate of regulatory structural cost.

Table 5-1 presents the calculated estimates of structural costs in the thirty-five regulated states. Due to the impact of advertising regulation on

Table 5-1
Estimates of Structural Costs of Regulation*

Regulation	Number of States Regulated	Total Sales (000) Q_1	Total Sales (000) Q_2	Cost of Regulation (000) $(Q_1 C_1 - Q_1 C_2)$	Cost of Regulation (000) $Q_1(C_1 - C_2) + \frac{1}{2}[(Q_2 - Q_1)(C_1 - C_2)]$
(1) Advertising Regulation	10[a]	2,850,014.70	3,340,568.20	$ 10,112.64	$ 11,087.11
(2) Physical Requirements	5[b]	(d)		1,996.76	
(3) (1) and (2)	20[c]	4,945,511.60	5,175,066.78	51,289.26	55,480.53
Total	35	$ 7,795,526.30	$ 9,055,634.98	$ 63,398.66	$ 66,567.64

*Costs and sales in 1970 dollars.

[a]Colorado, Georgia, Illinois, Iowa, Nevada, New York, Oregon, Texas, Washington, West Virginia

[b]Delaware, Montana, New Mexico, South Carolina, Utah

[c]Arkansas, California, Connecticut, Florida, Indiana, Kansas, Louisiana, Maine, Maryland, Massachusetts, Michigan, Minnesota, Mississippi, New Jersey, Oklahoma, Pennsylvania, Rhode Island, South Dakota, Virginia, Wisconsin

[d]Regulation does not affect sales volume; sales volume is therefore not presented.

establishment sales size, total sales in a state regulating advertising was over $1.2 billion less than it would have been in the absence of regulation. The total structural costs of regulation arising from a misallocation of society's resources amounted to between sixty-three and sixty-six million dollars in 1967.

It should be noted that these estimates are quite rough and probably understate the actual cost effects of regulation. This understatement occurs for two reasons. First, the census data upon which these estimates are based include only establishments with payrolls. Thus those establishments of the smallest sales volume are excluded from the analysis. The estimated impact of regulation on average sales size of establishments suggests that these small volume establishments may be more prevalent in states regulating advertising. The average sales size of establishments in states regulating advertising will therefore be overstated; costs resultantly understated. Second, the estimates are implicitly based on the assumption that the sales size of the included establishments (those with payroll) in regulated states is distributed normally around the mean. To the extent that regulation affects the distribution of establishment sales size such that there are more relatively small establishments, the estimates of structural cost will be understated due to the existence of proportionately more establishments with higher average costs.

**Structural Effects: Sales Size
Distribution, Organizational Form,
and Regulation**

Two structural variables, the distribution of establishment size and the prevalence of chain organizations, are hypothesized to be affected by regulation.

Sales Size Distribution

The presence of large establishments of five hundred thousand dollars or one million dollars sales volume constitute a major competitive element, affecting potentially the existence of smaller scale pharmacies.

Although there are no overt entry restrictions for large establishments, regulation may serve to effectively forestall entry by precluding competitive tactics (such as advertising) which are important in achieving scale economies or by making it prohibitively expensive (physical requirements) for large establishments to develop in or enter into the market.

Three estimates of the effects of regulation on the sales size distribution of large establishments were made. The first estimate was on the proportion of establishments with sales of three hundred thousand dollars or more; the second on the proportion of sales over five hundred thousand dollars; the third on the proportion of establishments with sales of over one million dollars.

The relationship was estimated in the form:

$$Y = g'(\text{DENSITY, PCPI}, R_2, R_3, R_4, R_5, R_6, R_8) \qquad (5.4)$$

where:

Y is the proportion of establishments in the sales size class

DENSITY, . . . , R_8 are as above

The results of these estimates display an interesting pattern (Table 5-2). For the proportion of establishments over three hundred thousand and five hundred thousand dollars, economic characteristics alone are significant predictors. Large establishments thrive in high income, densely populated locations. Of the two economic characteristics, population density appears to become increasingly important to the presence of the large sales size establishments. This finding may reflect a policy under which larger establishments pursue a progressively lower "low margin," higher "high volume" strategy. With such a policy, the number of buyers in the market area would play an increasingly important role. Alternatively, this relationship may indicate the development of more specialized pharmacies in richer markets.

Table 5-2
Regulatory Impact on Establishment Size Distribution

	Dependent	Variable	
	3 HUNDRED	5 HUNDRED	MILLION
DENSITY	.0013	.0010	.0010
	(1.93)	(2.66)	(2.88)
PCPI	.0085	.0030	.0010
	(3.3)	(2.41)	(1.91)
R_2	−.658	.090	−.440
	(.16)	(.03)	(.40)
R_3	−1.04	−.460	−.500
	(.20)	(.16)	(.35)
R_4	−2.03	−1.25	−.570
	(.25)	(.30)	(.25)
R_5	−.524	−.200	−.760
	(.20)	(.15)	(1.10)
R_6	−2.56	−.470	−1.13
	(.85)	(.34)	(1.48)
R_8	2.13	.092	1.88
	(.71)	(.06)	(2.41)
INTERCEPT	−8.8	−3.8	−2.1
R^2	.407	.386	.392

Regulatory effects, while insignificant in the estimate of the first two proportions, are in the hypothesized negative direction. The estimate for the proportion of establishments over one million in sales volume shows that two of the regulations, R_6, *Advertising Restrictions*, and R_8, *Regulation of Competing Distribution Methods*, are associated with the presence of these large establishments.

As with AVESALES, advertising regulation is negatively related to the presence of large establishments in the market and reinforces the premise that the ability to advertise prices is important in achieving scale economies. Physical requirements, regulating the distribution of physical store area between prescription and nonprescription products, or regulating inventory levels, also apparently inhibit attainment of large scale. The positive relationship between R_8 and AVESALES was found earlier, but the coefficient was insignificant. The regulation of competing distribution methods is significantly related to the presence of large establishments in the market.

Chain Store Prevalence

The prominence of chain organizations in retailing is potentially of special significance. As developed earlier, the establishment size of multi-establishment firms varies directly with the number of establishments in the firm. Thus larger firms (with larger establishments) are able to take advantage of scale economies. Secondly, chain organizations may enjoy economies in purchasing not available to smaller scale pharmacies, or follow product line and pricing policies different from smaller outlets. These characteristics bear a hypothetical relation to prices and thus the effect of regulation on the relative presence of chain organizations is of considerable importance.

Chain organizations are defined in two ways. The current *Census of Business* definition of a chain is eleven or more establishments operating under the ownership of a single firm. An earlier Census definition, and one still used by trade organizations in the retail drug market, considered a chain to be four or more establishments under single ownership.

Estimates in the form

$$Y = h\,(\text{DENSITY, PCPI}, R_2, R_3, R_4, R_5, R_6, R_8) \qquad (5.5)$$

where:

Y = The proportion of establishments belonging to a chain,

were made using as alternative dependent variables, the four establishment and eleven establishment definition of a chain.

From Table 5-3 the impact of population density as the primary economic characteristic influencing chain organizations can be seen. Chains, as well as large

Table 5-3
Regulatory Impact on Chain Stores

	Dependent	Variable
	CHAIN 4	CHAIN 11
DENSITY	.002	.002
	(4.42)	(4.61)
PCPI	.001	.001
	(.51)	(.52)
R_2	−4.62	−4.86
	(1.42)	(1.70)
R_3	−4.91	−4.18
	(1.26)	(1.20)
R_4	−7.53	−6.23
	(1.18)	(1.09)
R_5	−.025	.57
	(.01)	(.33)
R_6	−.796	−1.28
	(.34)	(.62)
R_8	4.46	3.69
	(1.94)	(1.78)
INTERCEPT	4.1	3.0
R^2	.439	.460

establishments, rely heavily on concentrated population to achieve economies of scale and organization. The regulatory variables R_2, *Pharmacist Ownership Requirement*, and R_8, *Regulation of Competing Distribution Methods*, are related to the prevalence of chain organizations. R_3, *Merchandising Prohibitions*, and R_4, *Limitation of Outlets*, were also negatively related to the presence of chain organizations, although "t" values are not significant at .10 level.

In those states where pharmacy ownership is restricted to pharmacists, a lower proportion of establishments belonging to chains (under either the four establishment or the eleven establishment definition) is found. The public health consideration leading to the enactment of pharmacy ownership laws, according to Fletcher,[1] is that nonpharmacist owners frequently force pharmacists to perform "unprofessional" functions. The economic argument for this restriction is that independent pharmacists must be protected from chain organizations and other potential discounters. Regardless of the motivation behind the enactment of such regulation, its presence has the effect of significantly reducing the relative presence of chain organizations in the market.

The regulation of competing methods of distribution, R_8, is positively related to the presence of chain organizations. When the distribution of drugs (either prescription or proprietary) can be limited to sale by pharmacies, the ability *ceteris paribus* of chain organizations to obtain a greater share of the market is enhanced due to the reduction in the number of actual and potential competitors.

Somewhat surprisingly, R_6, *Advertising Restrictions* is not significantly related to chain store prevalence, as it is to large establishment presence. This may be an indication that competitive strategies employed by chain organizations may be such as to offset the effects of advertising restrictions. These strategies, such as offering wide product assortment, locational choice, and pricing policies, may allow chains to achieve a discount "image" and thus overcome any disadvantages associated with the inability to advertise prices.

Summary

Regulation of the retail distribution of prescription drug products plays a major and encompassing role in shaping the economic structure of the market. Overall, regulation appears to increase the homogeneity of establishments supplying the market with respect to sales and organizational form. These effects are not without a cost.

The estimated structural costs resulting from restrictions on price advertising and specifying physical requirements for outlets increased the cost of distributing output between 63 and 66 million dollars in 1967. These estimates are likely to be understated due to the impact of regulation on the size distribution of establishments as well as data limitations; however, it is clear that the structural effects of regulation are a larger number of small volume, high cost establishments.

In the next two chapters, the conduct of competition and the impact of regulation on competitive conduct are investigated. Following this, in Chapter 8, the impact of regulation on prescription drug prices apart from the structurally, (i.e., cost) related impact is estimated.

6

Market Offer Variations Among Sellers

The previous chapter developed the role that retail pharmacy regulation plays in shaping the structure of the retail prescription drug market. The presence of certain regulatory patterns, notably those including restrictions on advertising, and competing methods of distribution, significantly influence the average size and size distribution of pharmacies in the market. Ownership requirements and restrictions on competing methods of distribution influence the organizational form of establishments. In this section an examination of the competitive characteristics of supplying market members is undertaken.

Introduction

This chapter serves the major purpose of describing differences in the characteristics of market members in terms of their market offering. By market offering is meant the mix of price and nonprice variables developed by the firm and evaluated by potential demanders.

The data used in this chapter are derived from a survey conducted by a marketing research firm for the *National Association of Retail Druggists* (N.A.R.D.) and the *National Association of Chain Drug Stores* (N.A.C.D.S.) in 1970. Elicited were comprehensive operating data from over nineteen hundred pharmacies nationwide. Preliminary analysis revealed the respondent pharmacies to be representative with respect to size distribution, organizational form and state location. Table 6-1 shows the distribution of sample observations in terms of sales size and organization. The majority of firms in the market operate single establishments, and the majority of all establishments in 1970 had sales of less than $200,000.

Organization of the firm and sales size are related. Establishment in firms of two or three units display larger sales volume than single establishment firms. Those establishments which are members of firms with four or more establishments tend to fall into the highest sales size categories.[a]

---

[a]The relationships here are consistent with those found in the 1967 *Census of Business* (see Chapter 3 for the distribution of sales size of establishments taken from this source) and those derived from the *Lilly Digest* for pharmacies in 1970. The *Lilly Digest* sample shows average sales of somewhat over $400,000 for all establishments and slightly over $200,000 for independent pharmacies. Fifty-three percent of independent pharmacies in the Lilly sample and 54.1 percent of all pharmacies in the N.A.R.D./N.A.C.D.S. sample have sales of less than $200,000.

Table 6-1
Descriptions of Sample in Terms of Sales Size and Organization: Number and Percent of Total Sales Size (000)

		< $100,000	$100,000-$199,999	$200,000-$299,999	$300,000-$499,999	$500,000-$999,999	$1,000,000 or more	
Organization	Single Establishments	265 (14.1)**	567 (30.3)	309 (16.5)	140 (7.5)	49 (2.6)	13 (.7)	1343 (71.7)
	2-3 Establishments	24 (1.3)	76 (4.1)	47 (2.5)	32 (1.7)	20 (1.1)	8 (.4)	207 (11.1)
	4 or more Establishments	22 (1.2)	59 (3.2)	60 (3.2)	66 (3.5)	79 (4.2)	37 (2.0)	323 (17.2)
		311 (16.6)	702 (37.5)	416 (22.2)	238 (12.7)	148 (7.9)	58 (3.1)	1873 (100)

*57 observations did not include information on sales size or organization and are not included in this table.

**Numbers in parentheses within the matrix refer to the cell value as a percentage of the total number of observations.

Briefly summarized, the survey collected detailed data on operating characteristics, establishment descriptors, nonprice competitive variables, price levels, and pricing policies. In the sections to follow we will describe and analyze differences in the market offering of establishments of varying size and organization. This chapter is, by nature, highly descriptive. It is necessary to draw out and develop the relationships of market offer variation in this manner, however, so that subsequent sections may use these findings as input into the analysis of market competition.

To facilitate the discussion an initial classification framework is developed to group characteristics of establishments in the market. This framework is shown in Figure 6-1, and consists of

1. Market Descriptors
2. Establishment Descriptors
3. Customer Services
4. Professional Services
5. Price Levels and Price Policies.

Market Descriptors

The economic and competitive environment of the firm affects competitive strategy. Characteristics of demand, and demanders, provide foci for the development of the mix of nonprice and price offer variations. Characteristics of competitors further describe elements in the market which each firm must continually survey and adapt to. Included in these market descriptor characteristics are the size of the establishment trading area, the number of competitors within the trading area, the income level of the population served, and the population of the area.[b]

Establishment Descriptors

These variables classified as establishment descriptors include elements which constitute variations in competitive strategy. Location of an outlet, for example in a shopping center or a medical building, certainly describes that outlet, but in addition gives information on the locational strategy of the establishment. Similarly, while establishment size in square feet conveys information regarding the physical dimensions of an outlet, this variable is also a good index of the assortment of products offered by the establishment.

---

[b]While it would be more desirable to have population density, this variable could not be derived from the survey.

	Market Descriptors (1)	Establishment Descriptors (2)	Customer Services (3)	Professional Services (4)	Pricing (5)
Sales Size < $100,000 100,000 – 199,999 200,000 – 299,999 300,000 – 399,999 500,000 – 999,999 $1,000,000+	Population Income Level Competition Trading Areas	Physical Size Product Mix Prescription Sales	Credit Delivery Operating Hours	Emergency Service Family Records Drug Information Library Waiting Area Compounding Prescriptions	Prescription Price Level Non-Prescription Price Policy
Organizational Form Single Establishment Organizations Multiple Establishment Organizations (2-3 units) Multiple Establishment Organizations (4 or more units)	Population Income Level Competition Trading Areas	Physical Size Product Mix Prescription Sales	Credit Delivery Operating Hours	Emergency Service Family Records Drug Information Library Waiting Area Compounding Prescriptions	Prescription Price Level Non-Prescription Price Policy

Figure 6-1. Framework for Analysis of Descriptive and Competitive Variations Among Market Suppliers

Customer Services

These nonprice customer service variables are indices of convenience and potential cost savings to consumers. The number of hours an establishment is open per week, Sunday and holiday hours are primarily shopping convenience variables. Credit and delivery services (the two most typical among pharmacies) also represents potential cost savings to consumers.

Professional Services

Associated with the prescription department are several professional services available to drug purchasers. Included among these services are emergency service for filling and if necessary delivering prescriptions at all hours, maintenance of a drug information library, filling prescriptions requiring compounding and maintaining drug usage information for purchasers and their families.

Price Levels and Price Policies

For the purpose of this analysis pricing strategies may also be compared between product groupings (prescription, nonprescription) as well as among establishments. The analysis of pricing strategy will focus on price levels in each of these two "product type" categories.

An index of the price level of nonprescription products is derived from the percentage of discount from list price which establishments offer on items in this product group. A measure of the level of prices of prescription drugs is derived from an index computed as a simple average of the stated selling price of ten different prescription drugs.

Initial comparisons among establishments classified according to sales size and organizational form will be made for variables in each of the categories detailed above. Figure 6-1 presents a matrix showing the primary variable comparisons to be made among establishments.

In testing for significant differences among establishments of varying sales size or organizational form on each variable, the Chi-square test of association is used. When both variables examined are ordinally scaled, the nonmetric measure of correlation, Kendall's τ is also presented. This measure of correlation allows a determination of the degree of correspondence between two ordinally scaled variables. As in the case of the Spearman rank correlation coefficient, the value of τ will vary from -1 to $+1$. The contingency coefficient, C, is a measure of association between discrete variables analogous to τ for ordinal variables. Like

τ, C will equal zero when there is no association between the categories under comparison. When there is complete association between categories, C reaches an upper limit less than one defined as $\chi^2/\chi^2 + N$. Values of C are directly comparable only when computed from contingency tables of the same size.

Market Descriptors

In this section the discussion relates to relationships between market descriptors and establishment sales size; market descriptors and organizational form. Tables 6-2 and 6-3 present the statistical results of this section of the analysis.

Population, Income, and Establishment
Sales Size

The presence of establishments with large sales volume is associated with high population density.[c] It is not surprising, then, to find large establishments most prevalent in cities with large population and thus greater market potential. This does not mean that small volume establishments cannot or do not exist in heavily populated areas. They can and do. Sixteen percent of the establishments in cities with a population of half a million or more had sales volume of less than $100,000. The positive relationship between sales size of establishment and population probably does mean, however, that establishments are unable to attain high sales volume in sparsely populated markets. Only 1.4 percent of establishments located in cities with a population of less than 25,000 had sales

Table 6-2
Relationship Between Sales Size of Establishment and Descriptive Market Characteristics

Variable	χ^2	d.f.	τ	N^*
Population	85.71**	20	.093	1904
Income	87.49**	10	.161	1902
Trading area	28.59***	20	.001	1899
Competitors	123.07**	20	.146	1898

*"N" changes due to incomplete information from respondents.
**$p < .001$
***$p < .10$

[c]The simple correlation between average sales size of establishment and state population density estimated from Census data was .497.

Table 6-3
Relationship Between Single and Multiple Unit Organization and Descriptive
Market Characteristics

Variable	χ^2	d.f.	τ	N^*
Population	51.99**	8	.103	1895
Income	44.08**	4	.126	1894
Trading area	9.29***	8	−.037	1890
Competitors	75.10**	8	.123	1889

*"N" changes due to incomplete information from respondents.
**$p < .001$
***$p > .10$

of over one million, and only 6 percent of establishments in these areas had sales of $500,000 or more.

In a similar fashion, higher levels of income are associated with the presence of establishments with high sales volume. Only 14 percent of establishments with sales of one million or more were located in cities where the mean per capita income was less than $3,000 while 54 percent of the establishments in the smallest sales size class were located in these relatively low income areas. Forty-two percent of establishments in the highest sales size classification were located in cities with per capita income over $3,450 compared to 22 percent of the smallest establishments.[d]

Population, Income, and Organization

Population and income characteristics of the market are also related to the presence of multiple establishment firms. In areas with populations of less than 25,000 only 12 percent of the pharmacies are members of firms of four or more establishments, while only 13 percent of single establishment firms are located in cities with populations over 500,000. With respect to income level, 51 percent of the single establishment firms contrasted to 31 percent of the establishments belonging to a firm of four or more units were located in cities with per capita income less than $3,000. Establishments of multiple unit firms appeared most frequently in the relatively high (over $3,450) income areas. Thirty-two percent of the establishments which were members of firms with four or more units compared to 23 percent of the single establishment firms were located in these areas.

[d]The simple correlation between average sales size of establishment and state per capita income derived from Census data was .452.

Competition, Trading Areas, and
Sales Size

Given the population and income characteristics of the market several other significant differences among establishments of various sales size categories are noted. Under consideration here are the characteristics of competition from other pharmacies and the size of the trading area.

Competition (defined by the number of pharmacies in the trading area of a given establishment) also varies considerably by sales size classification. While 13 percent of the smallest establishments reported no competitors, only one establishment with sales over $500,000 faced no other competitor within its trading area. By contrast 33 percent of the largest establishments reported ten or more competing pharmacies within their trading area compared to 6 percent of the smallest pharmacies.

In part the number of competitors faced by a given pharmacy will be explained by the absolute size of the trading area. We would expect the larger establishments, tending to locate in shopping centers, would report larger trading areas than small volume neighborhood located pharmacies. While very few (6.7 percent) of the largest establishments had trading areas of less than one mile in diameter compared to 18 percent of the smallest establishments, there was surprisingly little variation in estimated trading area size among establishments in intermediate sales categories. There was also little variation in estimated trading area size between the largest and the smallest volume establishments for trading areas of five to ten miles. Thirty-two percent of the smallest and 35 percent of the largest establishments reported trading areas between five and ten miles in diameter; 3.3 percent of the largest and 3.2 percent of the smallest reported trading areas greater than ten miles.

With the effect of difference in trading area size controlled for, a mixed picture of competition is found among establishments. When trading areas are reported to be very small (less than one mile) the smallest and the largest establishments report about the same amount of competition. However, for eatablishments reporting large trading areas of five miles or more, large establishments report significantly more competition. This relationship derives from the combined impact of population and location. Small establishments with large trading areas tend to be located in sparsely populated rural areas which cannot support several pharmacies. Large establishments with large trading areas are predominantly located in shopping centers in urban, high income areas. In such areas several shopping centers will be located within any five or ten mile boundary. Population is sufficiently large and income sufficiently high to support numerous pharmacies.

Competition, Trading Areas, and
Organization

Differences in competition and size of trading area between single establishment firms and members of multiple unit firms are similar to those among establishments of different size classifications. Single establishment firms report significantly fewer competitors within their trading area than establishments belonging to multiple unit firms. Eight percent of the single establishment firms report no competition compared to 2 percent of those belonging to multiple unit organizations. By contrast 20 percent of the pharmacies belonging to multiple establishment firms of four or more units reported ten or more competitors in their trading area whereas only 8 percent of the single establishment firms report this many competitors.

No significant difference was found between the size of trading area and membership or nonmembership in a multiple unit firm. A percentage of 11.6 of both single establishment firms and establishments belonging to firms of four or more establishments reported trading areas of less than one mile in diameter. Similarly 3.1 percent of the single establishment firms and 2.9 percent of members of multiple unit firms reported trading areas larger than ten miles. Thus differences in competition between single establishments and members of multiple unit firms cannot be explained solely by differences in trading area size. When trading area size differences are controlled for differences in competition become clearer. Single unit establishments with large trading areas tend to be located in rural areas, establishments belonging to multiple unit firms with large trading areas are located in shopping centers. Thus differences in reported competition between single establishment firms and members of multiple unit firms are primarily a function of location. Pharmacies located in shopping centers draw customers from a wide area. At the same time the greater number of shopping centers in large population, high income areas represent similar locational benefits for competitors.

Establishment Descriptors

In this section comparisons among establishments across sales size categories are made on the basis of physical size of establishment as a measure of product assortment, the mix of prescription and nonprescription sales, and prescription volume. The statistical results of these comparisons and those dealing with organizational form are found in Tables 6-4 and 6-5.

Table 6-4

Relationship Between Sales Size of Establishment and Descriptive Establishment Characteristics

Variable	χ^2	d.f.	τ	N^*
Physical size	1463.3**	25	.547	1889
Ratio of Prescription sales to nonprescription sales	527.9**	15	−.340	1875
Prescription volume	1063.5**	25	.508	1901

*"N" changes due to incomplete information from respondents.
**$p < .001$

Table 6-5

Relationship Between Single and Multiple Unit Organization and Descriptive Establishment Characteristics

Variable	χ^2	d.f.	τ	N^*
Physical size	290.02**	10	.214	1877
Ratio of prescription sales to nonprescription sales	141.63**	6	−.147	1854
Prescription volume	90.35**	10	.132	1892

*"N" changes due to incomplete information from respondents.
**$p < .001$

Physical Size, Product Mix, and
Prescription Sales Variations by
Sales Size

Data on product variety (the number of product items or product lines offered by each pharmacy) were not available directly from the survey. A surrogate measure of product variety is available in the form of pharmacy floor space square footage. That square feet of floor space is an acceptable, if less than perfect, estimate of the product assortment offered by an establishment has been demonstrated in several studies of retail markets.

Eighty-three percent of those establishments with sales volume under $100,000 have less than two thousand square feet of floor space. Differences between establishments in this sales size classification and those in the over $1,000,000 category may readily be seen; only 3.3 percent of these establishments are of such small physical size. At the opposite end of the size spectrum, no establishments in the smallest sales category were larger than siz thousand square feet while 87 percent of establishments in the largest sales category were over six thousand square feet and 50 percent were over ten thousand square feet.[e]

An examination of the proportion of prescription drug sales across total sales classification shows that total sales are inversely related to the proportion of prescription drug sales. No establishment in the largest sale size class had as much as 50 percent of total sales derived from prescription drugs. By contrast, 56 percent of the smallest establishments had more than 50 percent of sales derived from prescription drugs and for 47 percent of those establishments prescription drugs accounted for over 75 percent of sales.

This does not mean, of course, that smaller pharmacies dispense more prescriptions than larger pharmacies, but only that the relative volume of prescriptions sales to total sales is grester for these establishments. The modal class of prescriptions dispensed per day for the smallest sales size class is from 25 - 49. For establishments in the largest sales size category the mode is 150 - 299 prescriptions per day. Thus while there is an inverse relationship between total sales size and specialization in prescription drugs the relationship between total sales size and prescription drug volume is direct.[f]

Physical Size, Product Mix, and Prescription Sales Variations by Organization

Product assortment as measured by physical size of establishment is also related to organization. Single establishment firms are significantly smaller than their

[e]From the *Lilly Digest* data used in Chapter 4 similar figures may be derived.

Sales Volume	Average Square Footage
$100,000	1,302
$100-199,999	1,921
200-299,999	2,540
300-499,999	4,258
500-999,999	6,400
1,000,000+	10,482

[f]Once again similar relationships are derived from the *Lilly Digest* data.

Sales Volume	Prescription Sales/Total Sales	Average Number Prescriptions Dispensed Per Day*
$100,000	.605	31.7
$100-199,999	.504	53.0
$200-299,999	.448	72.9
$300-499,999	.282	74.4
$500-999,999	.213	111.1
$1,000,000+	.121	143.5

*Based on a 360 day year.

The simple correlation between the proportion of sales consisting of prescription drugs and average sales size of establishments as derived from the 1967 *Census of Business* is −.326. The Tau correlation for N.A.R.D./N.A.C.D.S. survey data is −.340.

counterpart members of multiple unit firms. Fifty percent of the single establishment firms are less than two thousand square feet in area compared to only 22 percent of those belonging to a firm composed of four or more units. Similarly only 5 percent of the single establishment firms are over six thousand square feet while 35 percent of establishments belonging to four unit firms are in this physical size class.

The mix of total sales between prescription and nonprescription products also varies by organization with single establishment firms specializing in prescription drugs to a greater degree than members of multiple unit firms. Forty-two percent of the single units but only 21 percent of establishments in a four unit firm report more than 50 percent of sales derived from prescription drugs. Prescription sales volume varies according to single or multiple unit ownership, but to a lesser degree than prescription volume varies with sales size. The modal class for the number of prescriptions per day dispensed by single establishment firms and members of multiple establishment firms was identical, 75 - 150 prescriptions per day. At volume greater than 150 per day, however, relatively fewer single establishment firms were represented.

Customer Services

In this section comparisons among establishments across sales size categories are made on the basis of customer services. The statistical results of these comparisons and those dealing with organizational form are found in Tables 6-6 and 6-7.

Credit, Delivery, Operating Hours,
and Sales Size

The customer services most commonly offered by retail pharmacies are credit and delivery. These services are "free" in that no explicit charge is made to customers for their provision.

Credit and delivery services of this type are most commonly provided by small, prescription-oriented pharmacies. Only 8.5 percent of the smallest establishments do not offer credit compared to 50 percent of the largest sales volume establishments. Similarly, 67 percent of the smallest establishments provide delivery services while 71 percent of the largest establishments do not.

On the other hand conveniences, in terms of hours of operation, can be described as a customer service which is a characteristic of establishments with large total sales volume. The number of establishments operating hours varied directly with sales size. Seventy-four percent of the smallest establishments were open less than seventy hours per week. By contrast, 60 percent of the largest

Table 6-6
Relationship Between Sales Size of Establishment and Customer Services

Variable	χ^2	d.f.	τ	C	N*
Credit services	307.12**	25	−.147		1711
Delivery services	143.55**	5		.267	1870
Hours open per week	600.66**	20	.411		1895
Sunday hours	350.38**	5		.397	1871
Holiday hours	325.51**	5		.385	1871

*"N" changes due to incomplete information from respondents.
**$p < .001$

Table 6-7
Relationship Between Organization and Customer Services

Variable	χ^2	d.f.	τ	C	N*
Credit services	146.1**	10	−.139		1703
Delivery services	72.9**	2		.194	1862
Hours open per week	79.3**	8	.139		1886
Sunday hours	62.2**	2		.180	1863
Holiday hours	80.9**	2		.204	1863

*"N" changes due to incomplete information from respondents.
**$p < .001$

volume establishments were open eighty or more hours per week and 5 percent were open over one hundred hours.

Similarly significantly fewer small establishments reported operating hours on Sunday or holidays. While 71 percent of the largest establishments were open on Sunday, only 18 percent of the smallest opened on Sunday. Almost identical figures of 75 percent and 17 percent respectively reported operating hours on holidays.

Customer Services and Organization

Similar differences in customer services and conveniences are found between establishments of single and multiple ownership. Ninety-three percent of single establishment firms offer credit services to customers. Only 71 percent of those establishments which are members of four unit firms report credit sales. While 75 percent of the single establishment firms provide delivery service, only 50 percent of the members of four establishment firms provide delivery.

Twenty-eight percent of the single establishment firms were open as many as eighty hours per week compared to 51 percent of four establishment firm members. Forty-four percent of the single establishment firms and 68 percent of members of four unit firms reported Sunday hours. Holiday operating hours were reported by 64 percent of members of four unit firms compared to 36 percent of single establishment firms.

The provision of credit and delivery services are characteristics of relatively low volume and single establishment firms. These services are relatively uncommon among establishments of high sales volume or multiple ownership.

Larger establishments and members of multiple unit firms display a greater number of operating hours per week than do small or single establishment firms. Similarly small volume and single establishment firms are less likely to have operating hours on Sunday or holidays.

Professional Services

Professional services as distinguished from customer services in general are provided to prescription drug purchasers and usually involve some interaction between customer and pharmacist. Like more general credit and delivery services, professional services are not explicitly priced. The statistical relationships between sales size and professional services, organization and professional services are shown in Tables 6-8 and 6-9.

The provision of professional services is felt by a substantial segment of the pharmacy profession to be an important aspect of drug dispensing and serves as a means of distinguishing prescription drug dispensing from a routine selling activity.

The primary professional services provided by retail pharmacies are emergency service (the ability of consumers to have prescriptions filled and if necessary delivered after regular hours in emergency situations), maintenance of a drug information library for pharmacist reference and so pharmacists may answer consumer drug-related inquiries, and the maintenance of family prescription records, which indicate the drug history of family members to insure that incompatible drugs are not taken together and to monitor drug sensitivities.

Professional Services and Sales Size

The provision of emergency services varies with the sales size of establishments. Seventy-five percent of establishments with total sales under $200,000 provide

Table 6-8

Relationship Between Sales Size Classification and Provision of Professional Services

Variable	χ^2	d.f.	C	N*
Emergency service	120.7**	5	.246	1870
Family records	48.1**	5	.158	1869
Drug information library	11.6***	5	.079	1870
Waiting area	8.9****	5	.069	1870
Acceptance of compounded prescriptions	3.7****	5	.044	1870

*"N" changes due to incomplete information from respondents.

**p < .001

***p = .05

****p > .10

Table 6-9

Relationship Between Organization and Provision of Professional Services

Variable	χ^2	d.f.	C	N*
Emergency service	59.6**	2	.176	1862
Family records	12.5***	2	.082	1861
Drug information library	3.2****	2	.042	1862
Waiting area	3.2****	2	.042	1862
Acceptance of compounded prescriptions	3.9****	2	.046	1862

*"N" changes due to incomplete information from respondents.

*p < .001

***p = .005

****p > .10

emergency service compared to 37 percent of establishments with sales of over $500,000. Similar differences exist with respect to the maintenance of family prescription records. Forty-three percent of establishments with sales under $200,000 maintain family records compared to 23 percent of establishments with sales over $500,000. The maintenance of a drug information library, however, varies little among establishments of different sales size. Sixty-four percent of the smallest and 57 percent of the largest establishments maintain such information for pharmacist reference.

Certain amenities associated with prescription purchases, such as the provision of a waiting area for customers to use while their prescriptions are being filled and the acceptance of prescriptions for filling which require compounding by a pharmacist, are not significantly related to establishment sales volume.

Professional Services and Organization

Establishments which belong to multiple unit firms provide fewer professional services than single establishment firms. Emergency services are provided by 74 percent of single establishment firms compared to 67 percent of establishments belonging to firms of two or three units and 52 percent of those belonging to an organization of four or more units. Similarly, fewer establishments belonging to a multiple unit firm maintain family prescription records (41 percent) as compared to single establishment firms (45 percent). Among establishments in multiple unit firms, however, those who belong to a firm of two or three establishments actually provide family records more often than single establishment firms. Members of firms with four or more units account for the greatest difference among organizational forms in the provision of family prescription records. Only one-third of these establishments maintain family records. No difference among establishments classified by organization exists regarding the maintenance of a drug information library.

As in the classification of establishments by sales size, no differences among establishments of single unit or multiple unit organization exist with respect to provision of a waiting area or the acceptance of prescriptions requiring compounding.

Price Levels and Price Policies

The discussion of establishment characteristics has to this point focused on descriptive or nonprice aspects of the pharmacy's offer. In this section, our attention is directed toward prices of both prescription and nonprescription products.

A detailed analysis of prescription drug prices is deferred until Chapter 8. In the present section we attempt only to describe differences in the level of prescription drug prices among establishments in various size classifications and between single establishment and multiple establishment firms. In a like manner the discounting practices of pharmacies for nonprescription products is undertaken.

Prescription Prices

The index used to measure differences among establishment prescription drug prices is the average of the stated selling price of the ten prescription drugs listed in Table 6-10. These drugs, which are dispensed with varying frequency for a variety of illnesses, were chosen so that the mean of the ten stated selling prices would constitute an index of the price level of prescription drugs for each establishment. Table 6-11 shows the distribution of the index over the pharmacies in the survey.

Table 6-10
Prescription Drugs Used to Develop Prescription Drug Price Index

Drug	Amount
Darvon Compound-65	# 12
Edecrin 50 mg	# 30
Erythrocin 250 mg	# 16
Ovulen-21	one
Raudixin 100 mg	# 100
Sulamyd Sod/Methyl. 10%	5cc
Synalar .03% 15 gm	tube
Phenergan Expt/Cod	120cc
Tetracycline 250 mg	# 20
Valium 5 mg	# 30

Table 6-11
Distribution of Price Index

Price	% Pharmacies
$2.50 or less	.2
2.51 - $2.75	.8
2.76 - 3.00	5.0
3.01 - 3.25	9.2
3.26 - 3.50	15.6
3.51 - 3.75	20.6
3.76 - 4.00	16.9
4.01 - 4.25	15.0
4.26 - 4.50	8.1
4.51 - 4.75	4.7
4.76 - 5.00	2.1
5.01 - 5.25	1.0
5.26 - 5.50	.6
5.51 - 5.75	.2
5.76 or over	.1

Grand Mean = $3.78

Prescription Prices and Sales Size

As with nonprice aspects of pharmacy market offerings prescription price levels vary significantly among establishments in difference size classifications. The average price level for the sample was $3.78 with an index for establishments in the largest sales size classification $3.31. ($F_{5, 1899} = 38.8, p < .001$) (Table 6-12).

Prescription Prices and Organization

The index of prescription drug prices also varied significantly between single establishment firms and members of multiple establishment firms. The index was highest for single establishment firms, $3.84, and lowest for establishments which were members of firms with four or more pharmacies, $3.55 ($F_{2, 1895} = 44.2, p < .001$) (Table 6-13).

Nonprescription Product Price Policies by Sales Size

Pricing policies for nonprescription products are determined from the stated discount from list price on nonprescription merchandise.[g] Discounting of nonprescription products also varies significantly across sales size classifications. Eighty-two percent of the smallest establishments compared to 7 percent of the

Table 6-12

Average Prescription Price Level and Establishment Sales Size

	Establishment Sales Size				
<$100,000	$100,000 –199,999	$200,000 –299,999	$300,000 –499,999	$500,000 –999,999	$1,000,000 +
$3.90	$3.85	$3.84	$3.69	$3.39	$3.31

Table 6-13

Average Prescription Price Level and Organization

Single Establishment Firm	Member of 2-3 Establishment Firm	Member of 4+ Establishment Firm
$3.84	$3.74	$3.55

[g]Respondents stated that nonprescription products were priced (1) at list price, or (2) 1-9% off list price, or (3) 10-19% off list price, or (4) 20% or more off list.

largest establishments reported selling nonprescription products at list price. Discounts of 10 percent or more on nonprescription products were reported by only 7 percent of the smallest establishments, while 81 percent of the largest establishments reported regularly pricing nonprescription products at least 10 percent off list price. Sixteen percent of the largest establishments reported discounts on nonprescription products of 20 percent or more ($\chi^2 = 441$, d.f. = 15, $p < .001$).

Nonprescription Product Price
Policies by Organization

Discount policies on nonprescription products also differed between single establishment firms and members of multiple unit organizations. Seventy-four percent of the single establishment firms compared to 39 percent of those owned by multiple unit firms regularly sell nonprescription products at list price. Substantial discounts of 10 percent or more were reported by 12 percent of single establishment firms but by over 45 percent of those belonging to a firm with four or more units ($\chi^2 = 207$, d.f. = 6, $p < .001$).

Summary

Significant differences among establishments of various sales size and between single establishment firms and members of multiple unit firms are found in the market. These differences occur with respect to each of the market descriptor, establishment descriptor, customer service, professional service and price level categories.

Establishments with a high volume of sales tend to be located in heavily populated urban areas of relatively high income. Their trading areas are relatively large and they face competition from a number of pharmacies. High volume establishments offer longer hours of operation than their smaller counterparts. While large establishments offer a greater variety of nonprescription products and lower prices for both prescription and nonprescription products they offer fewer general customer services and fewer professional services. Although the majority of large establishment sales are derived from nonprescription products establishments with high volume total sales dispense more prescriptions than do low volume prescription-oriented pharmacies.

Prescription drug prices as measured by an index of stated prescription prices are significantly related to both establishment sales size and organization. Establishments with high volumes of total sales and members of multiple unit firms have significantly lower prices than smaller or single unit establishments.

Nonprescription product prices measured by discounts from list price also vary in a similar manner by sales size and organization. Establishments with high volumes of total sales and establishments with membership in multiple unit firms report discounting and larger discounts than lower volume establishments or single unit firms.

Members of multiple establishment firms display characteristics similar to establishments of higher sales volume and to some extent this is due to the fact that members of multiple unit firms have a higher level of total sales. However, when differences in sales volume are controlled for, members of multi-unit firms tend to offer fewer services and lower prices than single establishment firms. Like high volume pharmacies they are more commonly found in high population, high income urban areas and located in shopping center locations.

Because so many significant differences between establishments in various sales size categories have been found it is extremely difficult to determine which of these many characteristics contribute most significantly to total sales volume. We cannot, for example, determine from this analysis the relative contribution of prices, convenience, or services to total sales. Similarly, we cannot determine which variables contribute significantly to prescription volume.

In Chapter 7 the descriptive analysis presented here is incorporated into a multivariate model of competition in the retail prescription drug market. This model serves two purposes: it allows an examination of the dimensions of competition in the market, and it allows an examination of the impact of the regulation of conduct on market competition.

7

Regulation and Competition: Dimensions of Nonprice and Price Offer Variations

Introduction

In the previous chapter an examination of market offerings found significant differences in the composition of the market offering among pharmacies grouped according to total sales volume and organization. In this chapter the findings in Chapter 6 are extended to examine competition in the retail prescription drug market. This examination will include an analysis of the relative contribution of each aspect of the seller's offer to sales volume and to the volume of prescription drugs sold. This analysis, in turn, is extended to examine the dimensions of competition in the market.

This chapter is organized in the following manner. First a model of retail market competition in the retail prescription drug market is developed. Data from the N.A.R.D./N.A.C.D.S. Survey are used to examine the structure of the model in a discriminant analysis framework. A major division in the analytical section of the chapter occurs with respect to a consideration of competitive behavior in this market prohibits price advertising of prescription drugs and/or prescription price based promotional tactics. In the chapter, therefore, price and nonprice offer variations of establishments in those states regulating price advertising are compared to those of establishments in states permitting such activity.

Our attention is focused on the following issues: Are the dimensions of competitive conduct observed among establishments related to market regulations limiting the dissemination of prescription drug price information? Are service levels, representing nonprice offer variations, "higher" or "lower" in states regulating advertising? Are price levels, representing price offer variations, "higher" or "lower" in states regulating advertising? As discussed in Chapter 2, proponents of price advertising regulations argue that price levels will not be reduced and service levels will be reduced in states permitting price advertising. We are able to discern three potential outcomes of regulation of price advertising. Our analysis will allow a determination of which is most characteristic of this market.

1. Regulation of price advertising is associated with a "lesser" degree of price competition. Prices are higher but service levels the same in regulated contrasted to unregulated states.
2. Regulation of price advertising results in a "greater" degree of nonprice

competition. Not only are prices higher, but service levels are higher in regulated states.

3. Regulation of price advertising results in a "greater" degree of price competition but price levels are not reduced due to the cost of advertising or promotion, and service levels are reduced.

Nonprice and Price Aspects
of Competitive Conduct

Variables encompassed by the term market offering may be conveniently dichotomized into categories of "price competitive" and "nonprice competitive." Price competition refers to the levels, distribution, and changes in the levels and distribution of product prices among sellers. While these variables constitute a major focus of many studies of retail market competition,[1] it is frequently the nonprice aspects of sellers' offers which receive primary attention in both popular and academic literature. Product assortment, convenience, quality, and customer services are typical measures by which market suppliers attempt to differentiate their offer from competitors and thus win sales and market share. The "sum" of all price and nonprice aspects of a seller's conduct constitutes his market offer.[2]

These considerations lead to the use of an "abstract product" approach for analyzing competition in the retail prescription drug market.[3] Utilizing this approach, the generalized capacity of the retail establishment to offer goods and services represents the "product" of retailing. The mix of price and nonprice offer variations represent the "characteristics" of the retail "product." As Baumol points out, most of the managerially significant decision problems of monopolistic competition are not treated in the standard models of the firm.

These models do not tell us how sellers deal with the diversity of consumer tastes that characterize most real markets and how, consequently, the firm decides on a competitive strategy that encompasses the specification of its products and the "marketing mix" that constitutes the distinctive personality of its selling effort.[4]

While no specific analysis of consumer behavior is undertaken in this study, the diversity in consumer preferences may be inferred from the diversity of the composition of the market offering among sellers.

The demand for the output of the retail pharmacy is a function of the characteristics of offer variation associated with the pharmacy, i.e., the valuation of each aspect of price and nonprice variation by consumers. Basically, consumers may be thought of as evaluating the offering of any establishment as:

$$u = f(p, s, A)$$

where u is a measure of utility, p is the price level of the outlet, s is the level of services provided by the outlet, and A represents all other nonprice offer variations which are not a subset of p or s. A simplified demand function for a multiproduct outlet might be expressed as:

$$q_1 = f_1(p_1, \ldots, p_m, s_1, \ldots, s_m, A)$$

$$\vdots$$

$$q_m \quad f_m(p_1, \ldots, p_m, s_1, \ldots, s_m, A) \tag{7.1}$$

where the sale of any item (and all items) in the establishment is a function of the price of the item, the price of each other item, the services associated with item purchases, and nonprice offer variations such as product assortment, location and convenience of operating hours.

Expressing (7.1) for retail pharmacies and aggregating prices and services by primary product grouping

$$q_{(p,o)} = f(P_p, P_o, S_p, S_o, A) \tag{7.2}$$

where:

$q_{(p,o)}$ = The quantity of prescription drugs, or the quantity of nonprescription products sold

P_p = The price level of prescription drug products

P_o = The price level of nonprescription products

S_p = Services provided on the sale of prescription drug products

S_o = Services provided on the sale of nonprescription products

A = A vector of nonprice offer variation characteristics.

This general model of demand for the multiproduct retail establishment is derived from Holdren's studies of market structure and behavior in food retailing.[5]

It should be noted that pharmacies may influence sales by the manipulation of one, several, or all of the market offer variables under its control. Over time the experience of competition will provide for management estimates of the sensitivity of consumer demand to variations in each. Thus the application of Holdren's work to the demand for pharmacy products represents both an empirical test and an expansion. The inclusion of specific product price levels and indices of product price, services associated with product and establishment, and measures of convenience and location allow the development and testing of a rather rich model of market competition. The interpretations of the results of our tests of the model should lend valuable insight into the dimensions of competition in the retail prescription drug market.

The demand for pharmacy products at retail is formulated as

$$Q_{j_{(p,o)}} = f'\left(P_{p_{ij}}, P_{o_{ij}}, S_{p_{ij}}, A_{ij}, V_{ij}, D_{ij}, C_{ij}\right) \tag{7.3}$$

where:

$Q_{j_{(p,o)}}$ = The quantity of prescription drugs sold or the total sales volume of outlets in size class j

$P_{p_{ij}}$ = The index of prescription prices for outlet i in size class j

$P_{o_{ij}}$ = The price level for nonprescription products for outlet i in size class j

$S_{p_{ij}}$ = A vector of prescription services offered by outlet i in size class j

$S_{o_{ij}}$ = A vector of general services offered by outlet i in size class j

V_{ij} = A vector of convenience characteristics associated with outlet i in size class j

D_{ij} = A vector of locational characteristics associated with outlet i in size class j

C_{ij} = A measure of competition faced by outlet i in size class j

Thus formulated,[a] the model allows a determination of the contribution of each of these characteristics and the set of characteristics overall to total establishment sales and prescription drug sales.

There is one additional advantage to the implementation of this model. This advantage deals with the potential value of the model to management decision-making. If the demand for pharmacy products in general is determined by a set of variables different from those which determine the demand for prescription drugs, we will be able to identify these variables. In doing so we will be able to identify dimensions along which competition for establishment sales and prescription sales takes place. Such findings may have major managerial implications for implementing strategies to increase the sale of major product lines.

---

[a]The rationale for classifying establishments into groupings of sales volume is twofold. First, the analytic technique of discriminant analysis which will be used in this section requires discreet groupings as dependent variables. Second, the survey data are such that no variable which might measure sales size is available meeting interval scale assumptions.

Testing the Model

The model presented in (7.3) is tested utilizing multiple discriminant analysis in a two stage process. In the first stage the criterion variable is the classification of each establishment into one of six total sales categories. In the second stage the criterion variable is the classification of each establishment into a category defining the number of prescriptions dispensed per day.[b] The predictor variables are the same in each stage.

$P_{p_{ij}}$ = Establishment index of prescription prices

$P_{o_{ij}}$ = Establishment discount policy for nonprescription products (a dummy variable coded 1 if nonprescription products are sold at list price and 0 otherwise)

$S_{p_{ij}}$ = Establishment professional services dummy variable

emergency service (1 if provided, 0 otherwise)

drug information library (1 if provided, 0 otherwise)

family drug records (1 if provided, 0 otherwise)

prescription waiting area (1 if provided, 0 otherwise)

V_{ij} = Convenience dummy variables

Sunday hours (1 if open on Sunday, 0 otherwise)

holiday hours (1 if open on holidays, 0 otherwise)

operating hours (1 if open less than 80 hours per week, 0 otherwise)

A_{ij} = Product assortment[6] (physical size) variable

D_{ij} = Locational characteristics dummy variables

shopping center location (1 if establishment is located in shopping center, 0 otherwise)

neighborhood location (1 if establishment is located in a residential area, 0 otherwise)

C_{ij} = Competition dummy variable (1 if less than three competitors are located in the establishment trading area, 0 otherwise)

---

[b]The groupings of total sales volume are:

1. Less than $100,000
2. $100,000 – 199,999
3. $200,000 – 299,999

4. $300,000 – 499,999
5. $500,000 – 999,999
6. $1,000,000 or more.

The groupings of prescription volume are:

1. Less than 25 prescriptions per day
2. 25 – 49
3. 50 – 74

4. 75 – 149
5. 150 or more.

Also included in the model are the population and per capita income of the city or town in which establishments are located.

The Discriminant Analysis Model[7]

A brief discussion is undertaken here describing the discriminant model, its formulation, underlying assumptions, interpretation, and significance. This is done for two reasons: first to facilitate the discussion of the results of the analyses; second to acquaint the unfamiliar reader with some of the characteristics of the discriminant model which make its use desirable.

The objectives of the analysis are:

1. To determine whether significant differences exist among establishments of different volumes of total and prescription sales over the characteristics constituting the establishment market offering.
2. To determine which variables in the set of characteristics constituting the establishments market offering account most for intergroup differences.
3. To determine along what dimensions competition in the retail prescription drug market takes place, and to discover if differences in the dimensions of competition among establishments exists in states in which price advertising is regulated compared to states in which it is not regulated.

The problem of studying group differences is one of finding a linear combination of attribute variables that show large differences in group means. The discriminant model derives the components which best separate the groups in "n" dimensional space based on a linear combination of original attribute variables (in this case variables constituting aspects of the establishment market offer). For each establishment a discriminant score, Z_i, is computed as a linear function of independent variables:

$$Z_i = B_{1i}x_{1i} + B_2 x_{2i} + \ldots + B_n x_{ni} + a_o \tag{7.4}$$

where:

x_{ni} = the ith establishments value on the jth predictor variable

B_i = The discriminant coefficient for the jth variable

Z_i = The discriminant score of the ith establishment

Most commonly, discriminant analysis is used for predictive purposes. The model is formulated and analysis developed to predict some nominal group membership based on measured attributes of an observation.

Recently another use of discriminant analysis has received considerable attention: structural analysis and the interpretation of spatial configuration. When used in this context prediction of group membership is not an issue. What is desired and required is a configuration which efficiently separates group centroids. This configuration indicates how the attribute variables contribute to the separation of objects in discriminant space.[8]

Discriminant Functions and
Interpretations of Dimensionality

The maximum number of discriminant functions or dimensions of the configuration (r) is: $r = \min (k - 1, p)$ where (k) is the number of groups and (p) is the number of variables. Since the number of attributes is generally larger than the number of groups the maximum number of dimensions is usually $(k - 1)$, as in this study. A linear combination of the original variables is derived that maximizes the ratio of among-to-within group variability. The first discriminant function has the largest possible discriminant criterion value and each subsequent function has a discriminant criterion value conditional upon those already derived. In this sense, discriminant analysis reveals the "dimensions" of group differences. We find simultaneously the dimension along which the maximum group differentiation exists; the dimension along which is observed the largest group difference not accounted for by the first; and so on. This process is similar to principal components analysis where the dimension corresponding to the first component has maximum variance, the second component dimension has maximum variance among those uncorrelated with the first. In discriminant analysis, the ratio of between-to-within groups sums of squares replaces variance as the criterion for determining successive dimensions. As in principal components analysis the dimensions, represented by the discriminant functions may be meaningfully interpreted. In seeking to interpret the discriminant functions, we attempt to determine which of the original "n" variables contribute most to each function.[9] Wilks Lambda determinant ratio statistic defined as

$$\Lambda = \frac{|W|}{|T|}$$

where:

$|W|$ is the determinant of the matrix of squares and cross-products of deviations of subjects from their group centroids, pooled over all groups

$|T|$ is the determinant of the matrix of sums of squares and cross-products of deviations of all subjects from the grand centroid is used to test the overall significance of the discriminant function. This statistic is distributed approximately as a Chi square with $p(k-1)$ degree of freedom. A Chi-square test is used to determine the significance of discrimination after the effect of the first $(1, \ldots, n)$ discriminant function(s) is computed. This allows a consideration for the number of independent dimensions along which group centroids differ significantly. F ratios test the significance of each independent variable controlling for the effects of all other variables in the equation.

Results

The analytical results are presented as follows: the discriminant analyses of establishments, grouped according to total sales volume in regulated and unregulated states, are presented, followed by a discussion of the derived dimensionality of competition in regulated and unregulated states. The second stage of the analysis presents the results of the discriminant analyses of establishments grouped by daily prescription drug volume in regulated and unregulated states and a discussion of competitive dimensions.

Total Sales Volume–Regulated States [c]

Table 7-1 presents the mean of each variable for each of the six total sales classifications used in the discriminant analysis of establishments in regulated states. From Table 7-2 it may be seen that the analysis resulted in five discriminant functions of which three were significant at the .001 level. This means

[c]States regulating price advertising of prescription drugs in 1970: Arkansas, California, Colorado, Connecticut, Florida, Georgia, Illinois, Indiana, Iowa, Kansas, Louisiana, Maine, Maryland, Massachusetts, Michigan, Minnesota, Mississippi, Nevada, New Jersey, New York, Oklahoma, Pennsylvania, Rhode Island, South Dakota, Texas, Virginia, Washington, West Virginia, Wisconsin. This list differs from the one presented in Chapter 3 due to the fact that Oregon repealed the regulation of advertising in 1966.

Congressman Benjamin Rosenthal presents a list of states restricting advertising as of October 1972. His list differs from the one presented above in the following manner: This study does not include the following states which Rosenthal lists—Nebraska, North Dakota and Vermont allow price posting, however Rosenthal considers them restrictive. This study does not. Alabama restrictions appear to be informal, no reference to advertising is found in the pharmacy board regulations presented by Fletcher. Arizona's revision of State pharmacy regulation did not occur until 1970. This revision apparently included a provision for advertising as Rosenthal includes this state as restrictive; Fletcher does not. Fletcher also excludes North Carolina and Wyoming from the list of restrictive states as does this study. Rosenthal includes Ohio and New Mexico as restrictive although no specific proscription on advertising appears in these states. They are therefore not considered restrictive in this study. This study does include as restrictive three states listed by Rosenthal as having no advertising restrictions: Florida, Pennsylvania and Iowa. Florida and Pennsylvania did not repeal advertising restrictions until 1972. Iowa apparently has a regulation prohibiting advertising. See: Benjamin Rosenthal, U.S., *Congressional Record* (March 19, 1973), H1879-H1898 esp., H1889 and H1897-1898.

Table 7-1

Group Mean on Each Discriminant Variable for Six Group Total Sales Analysis—Regulated States

Variable	Group 1 <$100,000 (203)	Group 2 $100-199,999 (464)	Group 3 $200-299,999 (256)	Group 4 $300-499,999 (152)	Group 5 $500-999,999 (85)	Group 6 $1,000,000+ (36)	$F_{5,1191}$	$p <$
Prescription Price Index	3.89	3.88	3.92	3.74	3.49	3.36	3.18	.01
Nonprescription Price Level	.82	.77	.74	.50	.28	.08	7.00	.01
Emergency Service	.70	.74	.75	.59	.40	.31	2.16	.05
Drug Information Library	.65	.68	.70	.70	.54	.69	1.18	N.S.
Family Prescription Records	.39	.49	.55	.51	.29	.25	1.97	.10
Prescription Waiting Area	.74	.71	.74	.64	.66	.53	1.36	N.S.
Credit	.10	.04	.04	.12	.35	.47	7.81	.01
Delivery	.65	.78	.80	.70	.42	.31	3.33	.01
Sunday Hours	.19	.37	.64	.76	.85	.72	6.37	.01
Holiday Hours	.20	.31	.48	.67	.84	.67	2.68	.05
Operating Hours	.93	.81	.59	.37	.29	.33	7.76	.01
Product Assortment	1.84	2.39	3.13	3.74	4.46	5.50	92.82	.01
Shopping Center Location	.05	.10	.25	.38	.60	.61	2.24	.05
Neighborhood Location	.53	.52	.58	.62	.67	.50	2.11	.10
Competition	.40	.41	.37	.29	.26	.17	1.62	N.S.
Population	526.00	428.69	346.18	454.93	546.33	232.53	.34	N.S.
Income	3,021.50	3,006.56	3,169.93	3,387.02	3,280.56	3,701.22	11.38	.01

Table 7-2
Characteristics and Significance of Discriminant Functions: Total Sales Analysis in Regulated States

Number Removed	% of Trace	Λ	x^2	d.f.	$p <$
0	87.4	.347	1253.61	85	.001
1	8.9	.827	224.51	64	.001
2	2.2	.944	68.25	45	.014
3	.9	.976	25.34	28	.446
4	.7	.989	12.37	13	.498

that the six groups can be described as being significantly different along three orthogonal dimensions. An examination of the F ratios (Table 7-1) for the independent variables shows that all of the market offer characteristics of establishments with the exception of the professional services: drug information library, prescription waiting area were significantly different among groups. Differences in the descriptor characteristics of population and the number of competitors in the trading area were also insignificant across sales size groupings.

The Dimensions of Competition

Table 7-3 presents the standardized orthogonal discriminant function coefficients for the three significant functions. These coefficients are used to determine the relative contribution of the original (significant) variables to group differentiation. An examination of the coefficients (analogous to factor loadings in principal components analysis) shows that the first discriminant function is weighted highly on the "product assortment" and "nonprescription price level" variables. This dimension may be interpreted as a *Merchandising* dimension and measures the variety and price level of nonprescription products. This dimension accounts for the greatest amount of discriminating power among groups. Establishments which have a large assortment of products priced at a discount will score highly on this dimension.

The second dimension, weighted heavily on "credit," "delivery," "Sunday hours," and "family prescription records" appears to measure a *General Services* dimension. Establishments offering high levels of general services will accordingly score low on this dimension. The third dimension weighted most heavily on "shopping center location," "operating hours," and "neighborhood location" appears to measure a *Convenience* dimension.

Figure 7-1 presents a plot of the six group centroids on the first two dimensions. These two dimensions account for 96.3 of the ratio of among-to-within groups sums of squares. Along Dimension I: *Merchandising*, centroids of

Table 7-3

Orthogonal Discriminant Function Coefficients for Three Significant Discriminant Functions—Six Group Total Sales Analysis—Regulated States

	Significant I	Discriminant II	Function III
Canonical Correlation	.76	.35	.18
Variable	Orthogonal	Function	Coefficient
Prescription Price Index	−.291	−.215	−.225
Nonprescription Price Level	−.523	−.213	−.114
Emergency Service	−.241	−.374	−.437
Family Prescription Records	−.052	−.530	.099
Credit	.540	1.580	−.166
Delivery	−.066	−.714	.525
Sunday Hours	.220	−1.289	−.093
Holiday Hours	.215	.479	−.988
Operating Hours	−.551	.354	.604
Product Assortment	.770	−.151	.445
Shopping Center Location	.255	.225	−1.049
Neighborhood Location	−.255	−.168	−.507

Discriminant Function I: Merchandising
Discriminant Function II: General Services
Discriminant Function III: Convenience

the smallest sales size groups are negative; centroids of the larger sales size groups are positive, indicating not too surprisingly that high volume establishments offer a wider variety of nonprescription products at lower prices than do lower volume establishments. Along Dimension II: *General Services*, however, no monotonic relationship is exhibited between the sales size group centroid and dimension coordinates. Both the smallest and the largest sales size groups score relatively high on this dimension indicating a relatively low level of provision of general services. The intermediate size groups, by contrast, are associated with the provision of the bulk of general services.

When the dimensions along which group differentiation exists are interpreted as variations in the market offer, these dimensions may be interpreted as variations in market competition. The fact that the groups are developed on the basis of total sales volume also imparts information as to the success of certain variations in competitive strategy. If total sales volume may be taken as any sort of measure of consumer preference, a larger assortment of products at discounted prices are preferred over the provision of services or convenience. Of

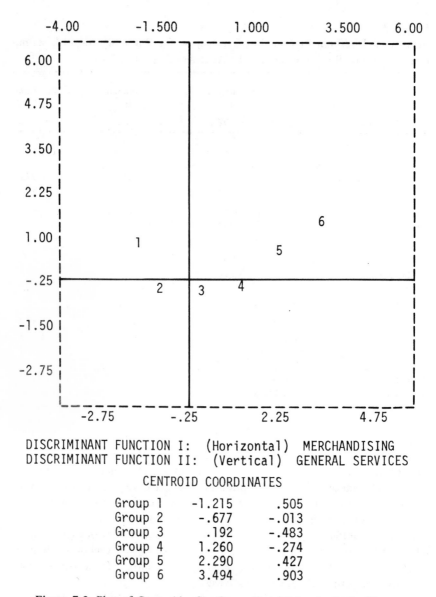

DISCRIMINANT FUNCTION I: (Horizontal) MERCHANDISING
DISCRIMINANT FUNCTION II: (Vertical)   GENERAL SERVICES

CENTROID COORDINATES

Group 1	-1.215	.505
Group 2	-.677	-.013
Group 3	.192	-.483
Group 4	1.260	-.274
Group 5	2.290	.427
Group 6	3.494	.903

Figure 7-2. Plot of Centroids—Six Group Total Sales Analysis—Unregulated States

interest is the finding that neither prescription drug prices nor prescription drug related professional services appear as dimensions discriminating among groups based on total sales. Apparently, in these restricted states at least, the pharmacy as a multiproduct retail establishment is evaluated overall in terms of nonprescription product and price offering rather than for its capacity to dispense prescription drugs.

Total Sales Volume – Unregulated States

Table 7-4 presents the mean of each variable for each of the six total sales classification groups in the unregulated states.

Table 7-5 shows that the discriminant analysis of establishment groupings resulted in five discriminant functions of which two were significant at the .01 level. In this analysis the groups can be described as differing significantly on only two orthogonal dimensions. An examination of the F ratios (Table 7-4) of the independent variables shows that only five were significantly different among groups. These were "prescription price index," "nonprescription price level," "operating hours," "product assortment," and "delivery."

The Dimensions of Competition

Table 7-6 presents the standardized orthogonal discriminant function coefficients of the significant variables for the two significant functions. The first discriminant function is weighted heavily on the "product assortment" and "operating hours" variables and is interpreted as a *Merchandising* dimension. The second function is weighted most heavily on "delivery" and "nonprescription price level." This dimension may be interpreted as a *Delivery Service* dimension. The weight of the "delivery" variable being over three times as great as the "nonprescription price level" variable. Figure 7-2 presents a plot of the six group centroids on the two significant dimensions. These two dimensions account for 91.4 percent of the ratio of among-to-within groups sums of squares. Along Dimension I: *Merchandising* we find results similar to those for groupings in the regulated states. Centroids for the smallest sales size groups are negative; centroids of the larger sales size groups positive, again indicating larger product assortment and longer hours of operation among high sales volume establishments. Along Dimension II: *Delivery Service* we find a relatively small amount of variation among group centroids. The fact that all of the other service variables were not significantly different among groups may indicate that this function captures a service dimension for these groupings. In these unregulated states as in those with advertising regulations it is the intermediate sales volume groups which are most associated with the provision of delivery service.

The dimensions discriminating among establishment sales size groupings in states regulating prescription price advertising appear quite similar. The primary dimension accounting for variations in sales size in both cases is one related to the merchandising function of these multi product outlets. The largest sales volume establishments score highly in both regulated and unregulated states on this dimension primarily through the provision of a large variety of products at discounted prices. The second dimension in both analyses is one measuring the provision of services. In regulated states several service variables contribute to this dimension whereas in unregulated states only "delivery" contributes to this dimension. This result derives from the greater variability of service provisions

Table 7-4
Group Mean on Each Discriminant Variable for Six Group Total Sales Analysis—Unregulated States

Variable	Group 1 $100,000 (56)	Group 2 $100-199,999 (141)	Group 3 $200-299,99 (91)	Group 4 $300-499,999 (44)	Group 5 $500-999,999 (30)	Group 6 $1,000,000+ (10)	$F_{5, 367}$	$p <$
Prescription Price Index	3.80	3.76	3.60	3.51	3.43	3.23	1.87	N.S.
Nonprescription Price Level	.82	.70	.62	.45	.20	.00	2.26	.05
Emergency Service	.84	.84	.75	.70	.50	.20	1.38	N.S.
Drug Information Library	.72	.62	.57	.61	.47	.40	.75	N.S.
Family Prescription Records	.38	.41	.44	.30	.07	.20	1.02	N.S.
Prescription Waiting Area	.70	.74	.68	.68	.73	.50	.55	N.S.
Credit	.04	.03	.09	.18	.33	.40	1.50	N.S.
Delivery	.70	.71	.86	.57	.40	.30	3.13	.01
Sunday Hours	.16	.30	.57	.75	.93	.80	.90	N.S.
Holiday Hours	.13	.25	.44	.66	.83	.80	.28	N.S.
Operating Hours	.98	.82	.57	.39	.27	.50	4.86	.01
Product Assortment	1.75	2.68	3.16	3.66	5.03	5.30	25.25	.01
Shopping Center Location	.04	.17	.27	.48	.67	.70	.54	N.S.
Neighborhood Location	.52	.43	.60	.66	.77	.60	1.41	N.S.
Competition	.52	.40	.35	.36	.07	.20	.81	N.S.
Population	132.48	92.18	164.85	148.61	234.57	232.10	1.11	N.S.
Income	2,704.16	2,661.54	2,978.36	2,824.43	2,884.80	3,232.50	2.22	.05

Table 7-5

Characteristics and Significance of Discriminant Functions: Total Sales Analysis in Unregulated States

Number Removed	% of Trace	Λ	x^2	d.f.	$p <$
0	84.6	.306	427.48	85	.001
1	6.8	.768	95.11	64	.006
2	4.9	.862	53.47	45	.181
3	2.7	.938	23.20	28	.723
4	1.0	.983	6.11	13	.942

Table 7-6

Orthogonal Discriminant Function Coefficients for Two Significant Discriminant Functions—Six Group Total Sales Analysis—Unregulated States

	Significant Discriminant Function	
	I	II
Canonical Correlations	.77	.33
Variable	Orthogonal Function Coefficient	
Nonprescription Price Level	−.505	−.507
Delivery	.065	−1.630
Operating Hours	−.779	.662
Product Assortment	.719	.179

Discriminant Function I: Merchandising
Discriminant Function II: Delivery Service

among sales size groups in regulated states. In regulated states a third dimension *Convenience* contributes to differentiation among sales volume groupings.

Service Levels and Price Levels

Do the levels of prices and the levels of services provided differ across sales size groupings between regulated and unregulated states? The answer to this question is equivocal. The prescription price index for each sales size grouping is lower in states not regulating advertising. Similarly price levels of nonprescription products (measured as discounts from list price) are lower in unregulated states. For the general services of credit and delivery virtually no differences exist between the percentage of establishments providing these services in regulated

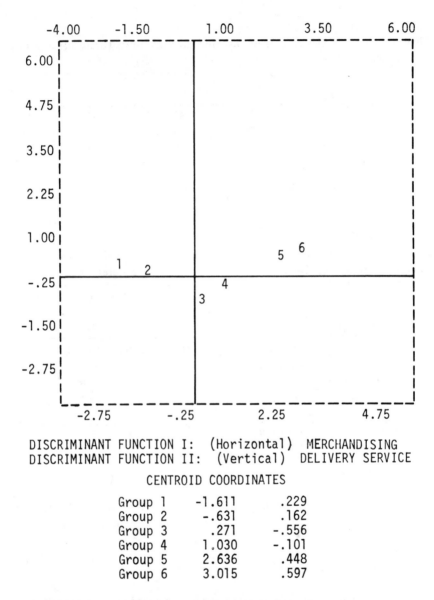

DISCRIMINANT FUNCTION I: (Horizontal) MERCHANDISING
DISCRIMINANT FUNCTION II: (Vertical)   DELIVERY SERVICE

CENTROID COORDINATES

Group 1	-1.611	.229
Group 2	-.631	.162
Group 3	.271	-.556
Group 4	1.030	-.101
Group 5	2.636	.448
Group 6	3.015	.597

Figure 7-1. Plot of Centroids—Six Group Total Sales Analysis—Regulated States

and unregulated states. Some differences in the percentage of establishments providing professional services are observed. A greater percentage of establishments in unregulated states provide emergency prescription services than in regulated states, but a smaller percentage provide a drug information library or family prescription records. The same percentage of establishments in regulated and unregulated states provide waiting areas for prescription customers.

Figure 7-3 shows how the price and service levels of establishments in each size classification differ between regulated and unregulated states. The graphs for the service variables may be read with the "Y" axis representing the percentage of establishments providing the service; the "X" axis representing sales size classifications. The "Emergency Service" graph, for example, would be interpreted as "In states regulating advertising, seventy percent of the establishments

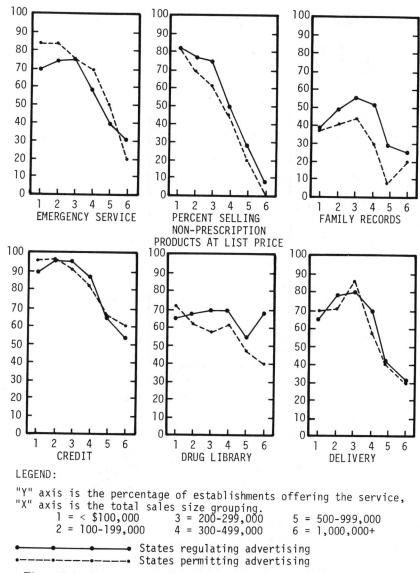

LEGEND:

"Y" axis is the percentage of establishments offering the service,
"X" axis is the total sales size grouping.

1 = < $100,000	3 = 200-299,000	5 = 500-999,000
2 = 100-199,000	4 = 300-499,000	6 = 1,000,000+

●———●———●———● States regulating advertising
●----●----●----● States permitting advertising

Figure 7-3. Service and Price Level Differences Among Sales Size Groupings in Regulated and Unregulated States

with sales of less than $100,000 provide emergency services; eighty-four percent of establishments in the same size class provide this service in unregulated states." The "nonprescription price level" "Y" axis represents the percentage of establishments selling nonprescription products at list price. The "prescription price index" "Y" axis (Figure 7-4) represents the average prescription price level of establishments in each sales size grouping.

Prescription Volume–Regulated States

Establishments in regulated states were regrouped according to daily prescription volume. Table 7-7 presents the mean of each variable for each of the five

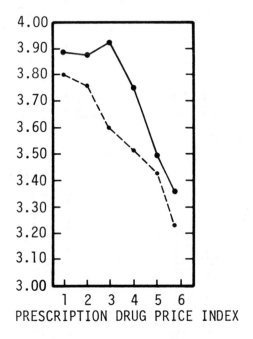

LEGEND:
"Y" axis is the prescription drug price index,
"X" axis is the total sales size grouping.
    1 = < $100,000   4 = 300-499,000
    2 = 100-199,000   5 = 500-999,000
    3 = 200-299,000   6 = 1,000,000+

•————•————• States regulating advertising
•—————•————• States permitting

Figure 7-4. Prescription Drug Price Index

Tal 1
Gr   Mean on Each Discriminant Variable for Five Group Prescription Volume Analysis—Regulated States

Variable	Group 1 <25 (62)	Group 2 25-49 (299)	Group 3 50-74 (389)	Group 4 75-149 (381)	Group 5 150+ (65)	$F_{4, 1192}$	$p <$
Prescr on Price Index	3.93	3.91	3.89	3.78	3.38	9.10	.01
Nonp ription Price Level	.73	.79	.72	.60	.37	2.89	.05
Emergency Service	.56	.72	.70	.66	.58	.56	N.S.
Drug Information Library	.58	.66	.66	.71	.68	1.53	N.S.
Family Prescription Records	.39	.46	.53	.44	.31	2.77	.05
Prescription Waiting Area	.47	.64	.75	.75	.66	7.92	.01
Credit	.19	.07	.06	.10	.26	3.29	.05
Delivery	.53	.73	.74	.73	.62	2.19	.10
Sunday Hours	.35	.42	.50	.53	.65	1.49	N.S.
Holiday Hours	.35	.37	.40	.46	.60	.98	N.S.
Operating Hours	.89	.76	.71	.59	.46	4.53	.01
Product Assortment	2.23	2.51	2.89	3.07	3.80	8.78	.01
Shopping Center Location	.15	.11	.20	.28	.40	1.18	N.S.
Neighborhood Location	.48	.51	.56	.60	.60	.70	N.S.
Competition	.58	.42	.38	.30	.25	3.91	.01
Population	432.79	431.44	451.31	390.24	587.53	.80	N.S.
Income	3,274.32	3,066.39	3,140.83	3,143.92	3,190.02	1.44	N.S.

prescription volume classifications used in the analysis of establishments in regulated states. Table 7-8 shows that the analysis resulted in four discriminant functions of which two were significant at the .001 level. The five prescription volume groupings may, therefore, be described as significantly different along two orthogonal dimensions. Table 7-7 also shows that nine of the fifteen market offer variables are significantly different among groups. These are prescription price index, nonprescription price level, family prescription records, prescription waiting area, credit, delivery, operating hours, product assortment, and competition.

The Dimensions of Competition
for Prescription Volume

Table 7-9 presents the standardized orthogonal discriminant function coefficients for the nine variables on the two significant functions. The first dimension is weighted most heavily on "prescription drug price index" followed in magnitude by "operating hours," "competition," "delivery," "nonprescription price level," and "product assortment." This dimension captures several attributes of competitive variation and may be most meaningfully interpreted as a general *Market Competition* dimension. Establishments with high prices (in both prescription and nonprescription categories), which are open less than eighty hours per week, offer delivery, and have a limited product assortment will score highly on this dimension. The second significant dimension weighted heavily on "credit," "prescription waiting area," and "family prescription records" may be interpreted as a *Service* dimension. Establishments providing these services will score heavily on this dimension. Figure 7-5 presents a plot of the five group centroids on the two significant dimensions accounting for 89.4 percent of the among-to-within group sums of squares. We find along Dimension I: *Market Competition* the largest volume group centroid negative; successively smaller volume group centroid progressively positive indicating that the smallest pre-

Table 7-8

Characteristics and Significance of Discriminant Functions: Prescription Volume Analysis–Regulated States

Number Removed	% of Trace	Λ	χ^2	d.f.	$p <$
0	67.3	.774	304.05	68	.001
1	22.1	.916	103.57	48	.001
2	5.7	.972	33.88	30	.286
3	4.8	.987	15.50	14	.345

Table 7-9

Orthogonal Discriminant Function Coefficients for Two Significant Discriminant Functions—Five Group Prescription Volume Analysis—Regulated States

	Significant Discriminant Function	
	I	II
Canonical Correlation	.39	.24
Variable	Orthogonal Function Coefficient	
Prescription Price Index	.877	.396
Nonprescription Price Level	.509	.385
Family Prescription Records	.275	.564
Prescription Waiting Area	−.679	1.044
Credit	.106	−1.682
Delivery	.526	.158
Operating Hours	.704	−.128
Product Assortment	−.371	.180
Competition	.570	−.419

Discriminant Function I: Market Competition
Discriminant Function II: Services

scription volume establishments are characterized by high prescription and nonprescription product prices, relatively few hours of operation, few competitors, and limited product assortment. The largest volume establishments by contrast are associated with lower prices, greater product variety, longer hours of operation, et cetera. Along Dimension II: *Service*, a now familiar pattern is observed which shows the provision of services associated with establishments of intermediate volume. Small and large volume establishments offer relatively fewer services than those of intermediate volume.

Prescription Volume—Unregulated States

Table 7-10 presents the mean of each variable in the model for each of the five prescription volume groups in states not regulating advertising. As may be seen in Table 7-11 only one of four discriminant functions derived from the analysis was significant in discriminating among groups. Of the variables in the analysis, only three were significantly different among groups: "prescription price index," "competition," and "family prescription records." These are the only variables in the analysis on which the centroids of the prescription volume groups differ significantly.

Table 7-12 presents the orthogonal discriminant function coefficients for these variables on the significant dimension. An examination of the relative

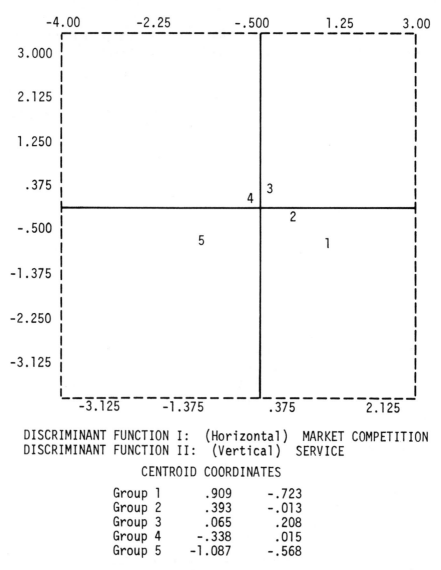

DISCRIMINANT FUNCTION I: (Horizontal) MARKET COMPETITION
DISCRIMINANT FUNCTION II: (Vertical) SERVICE

CENTROID COORDINATES

Group 1	.909	-.723
Group 2	.393	-.013
Group 3	.065	.208
Group 4	-.338	.015
Group 5	-1.087	-.568

Figure 7-5. Plot of Centroids Five Group Prescription Volume Analysis Regulated States

magnitude of the coefficients shows that this dimension appears to measure *Price Competition.* The "prescription price index" is of much greater magnitude than either of the other variables; the "competition" variable weighted approximately twice as heavily as "family prescription records." Establishments with high prescription prices, with fewer than three competitors in their trading area,

Table 7-10

Group Mean on Each Discriminant Variable for Five Group Prescription Volume Analysis—Unregulated States

Variable	Group 1 <25 (14)	Group 2 25-49 (89)	Group 3 50-74 (97)	Group 4 75-149 (138)	Group 5 150+ (34)	$F_{4, 368}$	$p <$
Prescription Price Index	3.91	3.78	3.68	3.59	3.43	4.53	.01
Nonprescription Price Level	.93	.72	.67	.53	.35	.79	N.S.
Emergency Service	.86	.78	.85	.72	.53	1.35	N.S.
Drug Information Library	.50	.63	.63	.61	.50	.35	N.S.
Family Prescription Records	.21	.46	.41	.35	.12	2.30	.10
Prescription Waiting Area	.50	.70	.72	.73	.65	.89	N.S.
Credit	.14	.11	.04	.09	.21	1.57	N.S.
Delivery	.64	.64	.75	.72	.56	2.06	N.S.
Sunday Hours	.43	.34	.42	.53	.65	.97	N.S.
Holiday Hours	.29	.30	.31	.45	.62	.36	N.S.
Operating Hours	.93	.81	.67	.62	.50	.83	N.S.
Product Assortment	2.14	2.52	3.04	3.30	3.68	2.27	.10
Shopping Center Location	.00	.13	.31	.32	.35	1.37	N.S.
Neighborhood Location	.29	.49	.55	.57	.68	.32	N.S.
Competition	.71	.49	.37	.32	.12	3.31	.05
Population	31.43	164.24	122.92	145.31	155.29	1.83	N.S.
Income	2,449.07	2,805.74	2,803.70	2,813.25	2,844.09	.71	N.S.

Table 7-11

Characteristics and Significance of Discriminant Functions: Prescription Volume Analysis–Unregulated States

Number Removed	% of Trace	Λ	χ^2	d.f.	$p <$
0	66.9	.679	139.67	68	.001
1	19.8	.873	49.20	48	.424
2	11.1	.946	20.00	30	.916
3	2.2	.991	3.38	14	.998

Table 7-12

Orthogonal Discriminant Function Coefficients for One Significant Discriminant Function–Five Group Prescription Volume Analysis–Unregulated States

	Significant Discriminant Function I
Canonical Correlation	.470

Variable	Orthogonal Function Coefficient
Prescription Price Index	1.069
Family Prescription Records	.477
Competition	.891

Discriminant Function I: Price Competition

and providing family prescription records will score highly on this dimension. As Figure 7-6, portraying the plot of group centroids projected onto the single significant dimension, shows establishments with the greatest prescription volume score lowest on this dimension, indicating low prices, a larger number of competitors and infrequent provision of family prescription records.

Discrimination among establishments classified by prescription volume in both regulated and unregulated states can be explained in fewer dimensions than can discrimination among establishments classified according to total sales volume. In both cases, the dimensions enable us to interpret differences in the market offer among prescription volume groupings. The competitive dimensions for establishments in states regulating advertising are considerably more diverse in nature than in unregulated states. In these, a single dimension quite clearly related to price competition differentiates among groups. In regulated states the dimensions of competition capture various aspects of competitive behavior including price, service, convenience, and assortment variations.

Service Levels and Price Levels

Do the levels of prices and services differ between regulated and unregulated states when establishments are grouped by prescription volume? The answer

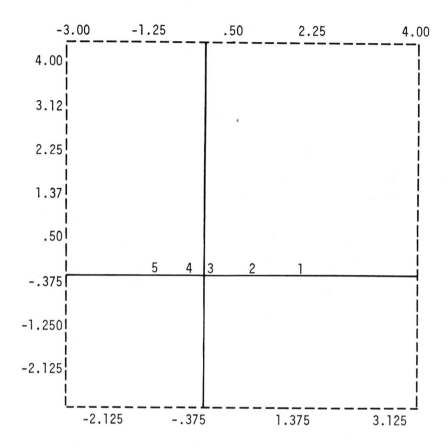

DISCRIMINANT FUNCTION I: (Horizontal) PRICE COMPETITION

CENTROID COORDINATES

Group 1	1.179
Group 2	.675
Group 3	.001
Group 4	-.324
Group 5	-.940

Figure 7-6. Plot of Centroids—Five Group Prescription Volume Analysis—Unregulated States

must obviously be yes, for when establishments are grouped according to prescription volume a pattern similar to that observed when establishments are grouped according to total sales volume is in evidence. (Mean price and service levels must be the same in both regulated and unregulated states for the observations have merely been rearranged by prescription volume.) Figures 7-7 and 7-8 show how the price and service levels in each prescription volume category differ between regulated and unregulated states. These figures com-

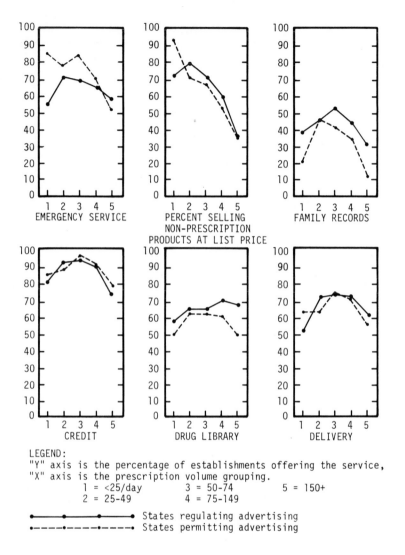

Figure 7-7. Service and Price Level Differences Among Prescription Size Groupings in Regulated and Unregulated States

piled in a manner analogous to Figures 7-3 and 7-4, allow an examination of the relative differences in price and service levels in regulated and unregulated states.

Summary

Price and nonprice variations in market offering are substantial in the retail drug market. There is great diversity in the number and type of services offered

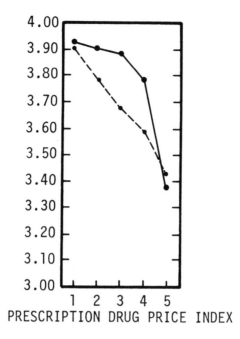

PRESCRIPTION DRUG PRICE INDEX

LEGEND:
"Y" axis is the prescription drug price index,
"X" axis is the prescription volume grouping.
   1 = <25/day   3 = 50-74   5 = 150+
   2 = 25-49   4 = 75-149

●————————●————————● States regulating advertising
●— — —●— — —● States permitting advertising

Figure 7-8. Prescription Drug Price Index

among establishments grouped according to prescription drug volume as well as total sales volume.

A model of competition in this retail market was developed from previous studies. This model incorporated price and nonprice offer variations to determine which variables or variations in market offer contributed to differences in total sales and prescription drug volume. The model was formulated in a discriminant analysis framework. This formulation allowed for an assessment of the dimensions along which competition in the market takes place and the relative success (in terms of volume) of variations in market offering. The analysis of the model was carried out for establishments grouped according to total sales and prescription drug volume in states regulating price advertising of prescription drugs and those with no such regulations. The major findings of this chapter may be described as follows:

1. *The dimensions which discriminate among total sales classifications are different from those which discriminate among prescription volume classifications.*

The total sales volume of establishments in the market is primarily related to the assortment of nonprescription products and the prices of those products—a *Merchandising* dimension. The second dimension discriminating among establishment sales size classifications is one denoting *Services*. Service provision of both a general nature (credit and delivery) and a professional nature (prescription records, emergency services, et cetera) are characteristics of intermediate volume establishments. General services appear in this dimension when establishments are grouped by sales volume; both general and professional services characterize this dimension when establishments are grouped by prescription drug volume.

2. *The dimensions which discriminate among total sales classifications and prescription volume classifications in states regulating advertising differ somewhat from those which discriminate among establishments in unregulated states.*

In both sales and prescription volume analyses, it is possible to describe differences among establishments in fewer dimensions in unregulated states, thus effecting a more efficient estimate of the dimensions separating groupings. When establishments are grouped by sales volume a *Convenience* dimension, related to location and hours of operation, significantly discriminates among establishments in regulated states. Natural locational monopolies appear more important in regulated compared to unregulated states in contributing to sales volume.

When establishments are grouped according to prescription volume, the dimensions discriminating among establishments in regulated states are *Market Competition* with relatively high weights on both price and nonprice aspects of the market offer, and *Services* with high weights on service variables. In unregulated states only one dimension weighted heavily on the "prescription price index" and "competition" and interpreted as a *Price Competition* dimension discriminates among establishments.

3. *Price and service level variations among sales and prescription volume groupings between regulated and unregulated states are mixed.*

Prescription price levels and the level of nonprescription prices are both lower in unregulated states. Patterns for the provision of services are virtually the same in regulated and unregulated states. The provision of general and professional services is primarily a characteristic of intermediate sales volume and prescription volume establishments. The provision of credit and delivery across establishment classifications is virtually identical in both regulated and unregulated states. A higher proportion of establishments in unregulated states provide emergency services than in regulated states. Relatively fewer establishments in unregulated states provide family prescription records or have a drug information library.

The regulation of price advertising of prescription drugs affects the pattern of competition in the market.

In some respects the results of regulation of price advertising are predictable, prices are higher in regulated states. In some respects, however, our findings are unexpected. Service levels are not uniformly higher in regulated states. Two service provision level patterns were higher, one lower, and two virtually identical to establishments in unregulated states.

While the present chapter has shown that prices are higher in regulated states, these differences are due in part, if not entirely, to differences in market structure and resultant average costs. In Chapter 8 we will examine the effects of regulation on prescription drug prices, controlling for differences in structural characteristics.

8

Regulation and Prescription Drug Prices

Introduction

In this chapter an examination of the impact of retail drug regulation on retail prescription drug prices is undertaken. In Chapter 5, *Structural Effects and Structural Costs of Regulation*, it was demonstrated that regulation has a role in shaping the structure of the market. The effects of regulation on structure are excessive distribution costs and waste in those states regulating price advertising of prescription drugs or regulating the physical characteristics of pharmacies. Consistent with these findings, the analysis of competitive conduct in Chapter 7 revealed prescription drug prices to be higher in states regulating prescription price advertising. In this chapter, the following question is analyzed. "What is the impact of regulation on prescription drug prices independent of the relationship between regulation and structure?" An alternative and more direct form of this question is, "Are there monopoly returns associated with regulation? If so, what is the magnitude of these returns?"

Analyses in previous chapters provided several indications that monopoly returns represented by higher than competitive price levels are associated with retail pharmacy regulation. First, conditions approximating those which would indicate entry barriers exist resulting from the regulatory impact on the sales size distribution of market suppliers. Second, the interpretation of competitive dimensions indicate that nonprice competition is the primary characteristic of establishments in states restricting prescription drug price advertising. In those states not restricting prescription drug price advertising, price competition appears to play a more prominent role in the retail pharmacy marketing mix.

The emphasis on the restriction of price advertising of prescription drugs which has developed during the course of this study due to the pervasive effect this type of regulation has on structure and competitive conduct does not preclude the possibility that other forms of regulation contribute to higher than competitive prices. As Benham has pointed out, "Many . . . types of regulations, if vigorously or selectively enforced, could reduce competition and raise prices."[1] Therefore, the potential for regulatory impact on price levels is not limited to an impact derived from restrictions on prescription drug price advertising. (For this reason, all eight regulatory categories are included in the estimate of regulatory impact on prescription prices.)

Estimation

To examine the issue of whether regulation is associated with higher than competitive price levels, a model is formulated incorporating variables indicated in previous chapters to be related to prescription drug prices in addition to regulatory variables. While the focus of the analysis is on regulation, the structural variables included in the model serve as a control variables reflecting variations in costs conditions. With cost related structural variations in price controlled for, the coefficients of the regulatory variables serve as estimates of monopoly prices attributable to regulation.

$$P_{p_i} = f(E_i, S_i, O_i, R_i) \qquad\qquad (8.1)$$

where:

P_{p_i} = Index of prescription prices of establishment i

E_i = Environmental characteristics of the market in which establishment i operates

S_i = Structural characteristics related to establishment i

O_i = Organizational characteristics related to establishment i

R_i = Regulatory characteristics of the market in which establishment i operates

Prescription Price Index

The establishment index of prescription drug prices used in the analysis is the mean of the ten prescription drug prices derived from the N.A.R.D./N.A.C.D.S. survey. In this analysis, the price index of each establishment is divided by the mean index for the sample. Regression coefficients, therefore, represent percentage contributions to the index.

Environmental Characteristics

To account for the exogeneous factors in the market potentially affecting costs and prices, variables representing the economic characteristics of the environment in which the establishment operates are included in the model. These variables are of two types: geographic and demographic. Geographic location potentially affects prescription drug prices in two ways. First, transportation and delivery costs may be systematically related to geographic location. Second, variations in the level and composition of economic activity may vary significantly by geographic location. A variable representing geographic location included in the estimate acts as a surrogate for variables contributing to geographic differences in economic characteristics.[2] Demographic variables included in the estimate are the demand related variables of income and population levels of the city in which each establishment is located.

Structural Characteristics

Structural characteristics included in the model are of two types: the general characteristics of sales size and the proportion of establishment sales accounted for by prescription drugs; establishment characteristics associated specifically with prescription drug dispensing. Sales size and the composition of output between prescription and nonprescription products previously were shown to be related to establishment costs. Characteristics specific to drug dispensing may be similarly related. In the latter category the following are included:

1. Dummy variables representing the provision of delivery service, maintenance of family prescription records, emergency services, prescription waiting area, drug information library.
2. Wage rate of employed pharmacists.
3. The proportion of prescriptions sold which are covered by private and public third party payment programs.
4. The proportion of prescriptions sold which are charged to customer accounts.

Organizational Characteristics

"Organizational characteristics" are a subset of structural variables as described below. They are presented as a separate component in the model because they have not, for the most part, been previously introduced.

Included as a subset of structural characteristics are variables which are either explicitly associated with multiple establishment organization, or variables likely to be associated with organizational form.

Purchasing characteristics. There are a variety of channels of distribution for prescription drugs available to pharmacies. Each has certain advantages of cost or product availability. In general, drugs purchased directly from manufacturers are available at lower cost than the same drugs purchased through wholesalers. Local wholesalers, however, may provide quick delivery or services not available to pharmacies purchasing direct from manufacturers. Pharmacies belonging to chains are often able to obtain drugs from a warehouse which purchases centrally for all chain members. Independents, in order to obtain any similar benefits from centralized purchasing may form cooperatives for purposes of buying and inventory handling.

Chain membership (four or more units). This variable is included to account for any economies of coordination and management not reflected in economies of scale or purchasing practices.

Regulatory Characteristics

The eight regulatory categories used throughout the study are included in the model.

R_1: Ownership prohibitions
R_2: Ownership requirements
R_3: Merchandising prohibitions
R_4: Limitation on outlets
R_5: Physical requirements for outlets
R_6: Advertising restrictions
R_7: Pharmacist restrictions
R_8: Regulation of competing distribution methods.

Results

Table 8-1 presents the results of the estimation. Although our particular interest lies in the significance and interpretation of the regulatory variables, the discussion of the results will proceed by variable grouping.

Environment Characteristics

All environment characteristics, geographic and demographic, are significantly related to the index of prescription drug prices. Relative to the geographic characteristics, all of the census region dummy variables display significant negative coefficients. Thus, the census region omitted is systematically related to higher prescription drug prices.[a] This indicates, perhaps, higher transportation and delivery costs in this area reflected in higher prices, or a relationship to some other regional characteristic not measured by this study. The coefficients for

[a]Whenever dummy variables are used in this manner, one category must be excluded to avoid singularity. In this case the excluded geographic area is Census Region IX (California, Oregon, Washington).

Table 8-1

Estimate of Relationship Between Prescription Price, Structural and Regulatory Characteristics

Variable	Coefficient	Significance Level
ENVIRONMENTAL CHARACTERISTICS		
I.*Geographic Location*		
Census Region I	$-.0822$	.001
Census Region II	$-.1587$	.001
Census Region III	$-.1274$	.001
Census Region IV	$-.1100$	.001
Census Region V	$-.0965$	.001
Census Region VI	$-.1087$	.001
Census Region VII	$-.1480$	.001
Census Region VIII	$-.0734$	.001
II.*Demographics*		
Population	5.27×10^{-6}	.032
Income	1.27×10^{-5}	.003
STRUCTURAL CHARACTERISTICS		
I.*Sales Volume*		
$< \$100,000$	.0883	.001
100-199,999	.0733	.001
200-299,999	.0659	.001
300-499,999	.0477	.001
500-999,999	.0175	.264
II.*Output Composition*		
(Prescription Sales as a Proportion of Total)		
$< 25\%$	.0098	.368
25-49	.0125	.147
50-74	.0021	.814
III.*Prescription Operations*		
Pharmacist Wages	.0081	.001
% Welfare Prescriptions	.0008	.001
% Charged Prescriptions	.0011	.001
% Prescriptions Covered by Private Insurance	.0008	.028
Delivery Service	.0307	.001
Family Prescription Records	.0170	.003
Emergency Services	.0022	.743
Prescription Waiting Area	.0061	.304
Drug Information Library	.0089	.124

Table 8-1 (cont.)

Variable	Coefficient	Significance Level
IV.*Organizational Characteristics*		
% Drugs purchased direct from manufacturer	−.0001	.686
% Drugs purchased through wholesalers	.0009	.571
% Drugs purchased cooperatively	−.0007	.045
% Drugs purchased through central warehouse	−.0002	.571
Chain Membership (4 or more units)	−.0201	.009
REGULATORY CHARACTERISTICS		
R_1 :Ownership Prohibitions	.0270	.007
R_2 :Ownership Requirements	.0120	.319
R_3 :Merchandising Prohibitions	−.0330	.420
R_4 :Limitation on Outlets	.0405	.110
R_5 :Physical Requirements	.0023	.753
R_6 :Advertising Restrictions	.0433	.001
R_7 :Pharmacist Restrictions	.0037	.681
R_8 :Regulation of Competing Distribution Method	−.0448	.001
INTERCEPT	.8165	.001

$R_2 = .375$
$F_{40,1808} = 27.14$
$p < .001$

population and income which are positive and highly significant indicate that controlling for other factors prescription drug prices are higher in high income metropolitan areas. The magnitude of these coefficients indicate that the effect of population and income on prescription prices is quite small—less than one-tenth of one percent for each thousand dollars of per capita personal income and much less than that for each one thousand increase in population.

Structural Characteristics

The coefficients of the sales size classification dummy variables indicate a significant relationship between establishment sales size and prescription drug prices. These coefficients display an expected result showing an inverse relationship between prescription prices and sales size.

None of the output composition variables (prescription sales as a percentage of total sales) are significantly related to prescription prices independent of other structural characteristics. This is consistent with the earlier estimates of long-run average costs which suggested that the higher average costs associated with greater specialization in prescription drug sales were primarily related to the functions and services of prescription drug dispensing. These prescription operation characteristics all display coefficients of plausible magnitude (generally less than one percent of price) and are in the positive direction. Thus the coefficients of the service characteristics may be interpreted as the "implicit prices" for these services which are reflected in prescription drug prices. Three of the professional services, "emergency service," "prescription waiting area," and "drug information library," cannot be said to have any significant impact on prescription prices. That is, these services are provided free to customers in a real sense. On the other hand the provision of delivery service is associated with a 3 percent increase in prescription drug prices; the maintenance of family prescription records is associated with almost a 2 percent increase in prescription prices.

Higher proportions of prescription drugs paid for by third party public and private repayment programs are also associated with higher prescription prices. This result hypothetically represents the costs of filing forms for repayment and long repayment periods. A similar argument may be made for the provision of credit services. Pharmacist wage rates also are significantly and positively related to prescription drug prices.

In sum, prior expectations that structural characteristics of size and characteristics associated with prescription drug sales are significantly related to prescription drug prices are reinforced. Prices are inversely related to sales volume; the provision of some nominally free services is reflected in prescription prices.

Organization Characteristics

Only one of the variables representing purchasing patterns is significantly related to prescription prices. Higher proportions of drugs purchased through cooperatives are significantly related to lower prices. Cooperative purchasing, as noted above, is a strategy used by independents to achieve economies in purchasing. Quantity discounts achieved by buying cooperatively can be passed on to consumers by individual establishments. The magnitude of the coefficient, however, indicates that the effect of this purchasing pattern on prescription prices is very small. Thus, either the savings in purchasing themselves are small, or the savings are not fully passed on to consumers.

Membership in a chain organization of four or more units is significantly associated with lower prescription drug prices. The coefficient indicates that controlling for all other structural characteristics chain owned establishments have prescription prices some 2 percent lower than nonchain establishments. This relationship may derive from quantity discounts in purchasing (regardless of source), economies of coordination and management, or, a "low" margin policy relative to prescription drugs peculiar to chains.

Regulatory Characteristics

Three of the eight regulation dummy variables are significantly related to prescription prices. All of the eight are of plausible magnitude of between 1 and 4 percent, six of the eight are in the hypothesized positive direction.

Of the two regulations displaying a negative coefficient, one, *Merchandising Restrictions*, is insignificant. However, the coefficient of *Regulation of Competing Distribution Methods* suggests that controlling for the effects of all other variables, this type of regulation is associated with 4 percent lower prescription drug prices. In order to interpret this result, it is necessary to recall some earlier findings.

In the examination of the structural effects of regulation undertaken in Chapter 5, significant findings were positive relationships between the variable representing *Regulation of Competing Distribution Methods* and:

1. the proportion of pharmacies with sales of one million dollars or more;
2. the proportion of pharmacies belonging to a chain of four or more establishments;
3. the proportion of pharmacies belonging to a chain of eleven or more establishments.

Those results suggested that in the absence of other types of regulation restricting the distribution of drug products to pharmacies would lead to an expansion in size of pharmacies in an attempt to achieve the benefit of scale economies, and to organize under chain ownership to derive economies in purchasing and organization.

An alternative to that interpretation is one that suggests regulation of competing methods of distribution was initiated by regulators as a result of the growth of chains and large establishments and therefore the enactment of such regulation represents the attempt to limit any further sources of competition to independent pharmacies.[3]

The regression estimate above includes sales size variables and a variable representing the membership of an establishment in a chain of four or more pharmacies. Unfortunately, however, the survey data did not allow the inclusion of a variable representing the membership of an establishment in a chain of eleven or more pharmacies. Therefore, the direction and magnitude of the *Regulation of Competing Distribution Methods* variable indicate it is picking up the price effect of an unmeasured characteristic—membership in a chain of eleven or more pharmacies. If this is the case, such establishments exhibit prescription drug prices slightly over 4 percent lower than nonchain or small chain establishments.

Two regulations are associated with significantly higher drug prices: *Ownership Prohibitions* and *Advertising Restrictions*. Of these two, the impact of the advertising restriction is by far the greater, due both to the size of the coefficient and the number of states having enacted advertising restrictions. The coefficient estimate of the *Ownership Prohibition* variable indicates that in states with such regulation, prescription prices are 2.7 percent higher than in states without such regulation.[b] Where price advertising of prescription drugs is prohibited, the estimate indicates that prescription prices are higher by 4.3 percent than in states not regulating advertising.[c]

The Magnitude of Price Effects

From the regression estimates presented above, an estimate of the magnitude of the monopoly returns attributable to regulation may be derived. This may be accomplished by multiplying the coefficient of R_1, *Ownership Prohibitions*, and R_6, *Advertising Restrictions*, by the volume of prescription sales in states having either or both those regulations.

Unfortunately there are no available data on prescription sales volume or the number of prescriptions dispensed in any but aggregate form. (An exception to this statement is the estimate of unit prescription volume by state presented in a special section of the *Census of Business—1967* dealing with retail pharmacies.)

Therefore it is necessary to estimate prescription drug sales volume or unit volume by state. Both sales volume and unit volume by state are estimated for this study. The computation of both of these bases is undertaken primarily to determine how sensitive the estimates of monopoly returns are to the base used. Given these bases are computed from independent sources the more similar the estimates of monopoly returns computed from these figures the more confidence we might put in them. Table 8-2 presents the computed sales and unit volume figures for 1970.

The Social Security Administration estimated prescription expenditures of $4.4 billion for calendar 1970 and $4.2 billion for fiscal 1970.[4] Thus the calculated $4.025 billion presented here as an estimate of prescription sales appears reasonably accurate. The estimate of the unit volume may be even more accurate since it is unlikely that the distribution of prescription unit volume among states would be subject to substantial change over the period 1967-1970.

The total monopoly returns attributable to regulation based on the prescrip-

[b]States having enacted the *Ownership Prohibitions* regulation are California, Maryland, Pennsylvania, Colorado, Mississippi, and Utah.

[c]Ninety-five percent confidence interval for *Advertising Restrictions* is 2.7 - 5.97 percent. Ninety-five percent confidence interval for *Ownership Prohibitions* is .73 - 4.6 percent.

Table 8-2

Total Sales Volume, Estimated Prescription Sales Volume, Estimated Prescriptions Dispensed 1970, by State

State	Total Sales Volume[1] (000)	Prescription Sales Volume[2] (000)	Prescriptions Dispensed[3] (000)
Alabama	$ 165,196	$ 70,538.69	19,152.00
Arizona	149,930	34,184.04	9,156.48
Arkansas	98,528	42,465.57	14,823.04
California	1,642,562	446,487.61	111,993.60
Colorado	159,564	42,603.59	14,543.36
Connecticut	187,854	62,931.09	19,431.68
Delaware	28,634	8,876.54	2,492.80
District of Columbia	118,621	24,791.79	7,648.64
Florida	570,950	167,859.30	42,851.84
Georgia	264,490	99,183.75	26,071.04
Idaho	53,034	14,690.42	5,399.04
Illinois	852,987	215,805.71	75,975.68
Indiana	371,195	106,161.77	31,153.92
Iowa	174,408	53,543.26	15,662.08
Kansas	137,463	48,524.44	14,823.04
Kentucky	198,085	66,754.66	18,993.92
Louisiana	196,324	69,106.05	22,167.68
Maine	44,413	18,342.57	5,289.60
Maryland	307,650	69,836.55	20,781.44
Massachusetts	352,824	125,252,52	37,379.84
Michigan	596,971	164,764.00	49,965.44
Minnesota	221,304	64,842.07	21,936.64
Mississippi	96,269	38,988.95	13,607.04
Missouri	342,149	104,355.45	28,393.60
Montana	51,615	12,955.37	3,489.92
Nebraska	97,746	17,713.36	8,791.68
Nevada	53,034	11,720.51	2,213.12
New Hampshire	29,846	13,012.86	4,134.40
New Jersey	372,613	121,099.23	39,155.20
New Mexico	59,425	17,470.95	5,739.52
New York	980,684	311,857.51	97,048.96
North Carolina	278,509	119,480.36	39,167.36
North Dakota	40,822	12,164.96	3,818.24

Table 8-2 (cont.)

State	Total Sales Volume[1] (000)	Prescription Sales Volume[2] (000)	Prescriptions Dispensed[3] (000)
Ohio	634,646	201,817.43	59,839.36
Oklahoma	142,184	60,286.02	14,750.08
Oregon	140,079	36,280.46	11,661.44
Pennsylvania	605,195	223,316.96	69,676.80
Rhode Island	60,382	22,462.10	6,736.64
South Carolina	128,824	50,499.01	17,571.20
South Dakota	50,058	13,312.77	3,550.72
Tennessee	227,676	80,369.63	28,576.00
Texas	664,772	253,942.90	77,994.24
Utah	101,320	18,642.88	5,654.40
Vermont	19,720	7,651.36	2,577.90
Virginia	303,697	82,605.58	28,369.28
Washington	241,957	65,812.23	17,656.32
West Virginia	84,900	33,875.10	11,284.48
Wisconsin	227,120	69,498.72	23,286.40
Wyoming	26.266	6,356.37	1,629.44
Total (000)	$12,963,485	$4,025,125	1,214,067

Notes:

[1] Total Sales of Pharmacies from *1971 Survey of Buying Power* (New York: Sales Management, Inc., July 10, 1971), p. B-6 © 1971, Sales Management Survey of Buying Power; further reproduction is forbidden.

[2] Total Prescription Sales derived by applying the ratio of prescription sales to total sales for each state (*Census of Business 1967–Retail Trade Reports*) to the 1970 total sales estimate.

[3] Total Number of Prescriptions Dispensed by State was derived from taking the total number of prescriptions dispensed at retail (*Prescription Drug Data Summary 1972*, Department of Health, Education and Welfare # (SSA) 73-11900 U.S. Government Printing Office) and assuming the relative volume of each state in 1970 was the same as the relative volume in 1967.

tion sales volume estimate was derived by simply multiplying the regression coefficient of R_1, *Ownership Prohibitions*, by the sales volume of states with R_1; multiplying the regression coefficient of R_6, *Advertising Restrictions*, by the sales volume of states with R_6, and summing. The total monopoly returns attributable to regulation based on the number of prescriptions dispensed was estimated in a similar manner after converting the regression coefficients from percentage figures to dollar figures.

The estimates computed from these two bases (Table 8-2) are of comparable magnitude. The figures indicate that prescription drug purchasers paid over $150 million in monopoly prices in 1970 in states regulating advertising and ownership. The major contributor to this figure is regulation of price advertising. Monopoly returns attributable to advertising restrictions account for 86 percent of total estimated monopoly returns (Table 8-3).

Regulation and Prescription Drug Consumption

A major controversy regarding the regulation of price advertising of prescription drugs involves the effect that such regulation has on prescription drug consumption. In Chapter 2 it was noted that an argument for maintaining advertising restrictions is that price advertising encourages the consumption of prescription drugs. Such consumption, stimulated by advertising is viewed as abusive.[d] This line of argument would suggest that per capita prescription drug consumption is greater in states not regulating advertising. It is not an argument in accordance with the one proposed in Chapter 5 of this study. At that time it was suggested that pharmacies individually or collectively could not increase aggregate demand for prescription drugs since demand is derived from the health status of individuals and subject to the discretionary behavior of prescribers.

Table 8-3
Estimates of Price Effects of Regulation: Ownership Prohibitions and Advertising Restrictions

Regulation	(Base) Sales Volume	(Base) Unit Volume
Ownership Prohibitions	$ 22,676,410	$ 24,098,177
Advertising Restrictions	134,510,930	152,409,278
Total	$157,187,340	$176,507,455

[d]It should be noted that should the absence of a regulation restricting advertising be positively associated with prescription drug consumption this may represent a socially beneficial effect. This would be the case if price information increased the propensity of individuals to fill a prescription once written for them. An examination of this issue could only be carried out by comparing the ratio of prescriptions written to prescriptions filled in states restricting price advertising and in unrestricted states. Unfortunately no figures exist allowing such a comparison.

The hypothesis that the absence of prescription price advertising regulation has no effect on consumption can be tested by estimating a function in the following form:

$$PERCAP = f'(P, PCPI, R_6, MD)$$

where:

PERCAP = State per capita prescription drug consumption in 1970

P = Price index for each state derived from the 1970 N.A.R.D./ N.A.C.D.S. Survey (Table 8-4)

R_6 = Advertising dummy variable (1 if state has advertising regulation, 0 otherwise)

MD = The number of prescribers (physicians, dentists, osteopaths) per capita 1970

Alternative functional forms included two additional variables: the proportion of state population over sixty-five and the number of pharmacies per capita. The proportion of state population over sixty-five was included due to the incidence of illness and resultant prescription drug usage experienced by this segment. This variable was never significant. The number of pharmacies per capita was included in one estimate and while the coefficient was positive and significantly related to per capita consumption it was felt that the direction of causation was likely to be reversed, i.e., the number of pharmacies per capita is a function of the demand for prescription drugs rather than the other way around.

In terms of variance explained the results of the estimates were poor. The highest R^2 obtained was .121 ($F = .966, p > .25$) and this was with all variables including the proportion of elderly population and pharmacies per capita. In terms of information regarding relationships among variables, however, the estimates were useful. Four findings are of particular interest:

1. Per capita income is positively and significantly related to per capita prescription consumption. Income elasticity ranged from .11 to .29 depending on the form of the equation.
2. Price is not significantly related to per capita prescription consumption. Elasticity estimates ranged from $-.29$ to $-.41$ depending on the form of the equation. However, the insignificance of price in the equation suggests elasticity may be very close to zero.
3. Price advertising restrictions are not significantly related to per capita prescription consumption regardless of the form of the equation. The coefficient of this variable was never significant at even the .50 level.
4. No consistent relationship was found between the number of prescribers per

Table 8-4
Prescription Price Index by State

State	Index
Alabama	3.568
Arizona	3.401
Arkansas	3.781
California	4.478
Colorado	3.876
Connecticut	4.076
Delaware	3.298
District of Colombia	3.786
Florida	3.641
Georgia	3.732
Idaho	3.827
Illinois	3.867
Indiana	3.338
Iowa	3.801
Kansas	3.817
Kentucky	3.776
Louisiana	3.622
Maine	3.775
Maryland	3.612
Massachusetts	3.909
Michigan	3.770
Minnesota	3.692
Mississippi	3.621
Missouri	3.742
Montana	3.786
Nebraska	3.679
Nevada	4.488
New Hampshire	3.817
New Jersey	4.053
New Mexico	4.085
New York	3.737
North Carolina	3.537
North Dakota	3.590
Ohio	3.522
Oklahoma	3.525
Oregon	3.672
Pennsylvania	3.589
Rhode Island	3.065
South Carolina	3.766
South Dakota	3.672

Table 8-4 (cont.)

State	Index
Tennessee	3.591
Texas	3.783
Utah	3.764
Vermont	3.466
Virginia	3.632
Washington	4.068
West Virginia	3.547
Wisconsin	3.710
Wyoming	3.815

capita and per capita prescription drug consumption. It is highly probable that the high correlation between this variable and per capita income contributed to instability.

In conclusion, then, the regulation of price advertising has no effect on per capita prescription drug consumption and demand appears to be highly price and income inelastic.

Summary

The purpose of this chapter has been to determine if there are monopoly returns associated with regulation. A model was formulated incorporating correlates of establishment costs, exogeneous market characteristics, organizational character-istics, and regulatory variables. Estimates indicated results highly consistent with analyses in previous chapters. *Restrictions on Advertising* and *Ownership Prohibitions* result in monopoly returns estimated at between $156 and $176 million, or about 4 percent of total prescription sales. These returns take the form of an income transfer, in the form of higher prices, from drug purchasers to retail sellers.

Per capita prescription drug consumption was found to be highly price inelastic, income inelastic and unrelated to advertising restrictions.

9

Summary and Implications

The major questions this study has sought to answer are three: What is the effect of public policy, represented by state regulation, on the structure of the retail market for prescription drugs? What is the effect of public policy on the conduct of competition in the market? What are the effects of market structure and competitive conduct on consumer prescription drug prices? In this chapter a summary of the particular findings of the study is presented.

Structure

The supply structure of the retail prescription drug market is characterized by small volume, independently-owned pharmacies. Relative to pharmacies belonging to chain organizations independents have smaller sales volume and tend to specialize in the sale of prescription drugs. This structure is, however, evolving into one in which the large multiproduct pharmacy plays a more prominent role. A significant trend in market structure is an increasing share of total pharmacy sales accounted for by a relatively small number of large independent and chain pharmacies. Bucklin notes,

In the drugstore trade, for example, new establishments are being constructed that are capable of doing all the business of small cities of around 25,000 - 35,000 population. Although such stores are not yet common and carry lines of merchandise far beyond those handled by the typical drugstore—indeed they verge on being general-merchandise establishments—the impact is nevertheless to bring a greater proportion of prescription volume into fewer hands.[1]

One primary reason for this trend is the existence of significant operating economies in prescription drug retailing. These economies exist with respect to scale (which contributes to an explanation of the trend of increasing pharmacy size), and with respect to output composition (which contributes to an explanation of the trend of a general expansion of wider product assortment).

Regulation and Structure

Structural characteristics of the market—sales size of establishments, the sales size distribution of establishments, the composition of output between prescription drugs and nonprescription products, the organization of establishments under multiple ownership—are significantly and primarily related to economic characteristics of the market. Population levels, population density and per capita income are variables contributing to the pattern of supply structure characteristics observed in the market. Larger and fewer pharmacies and pharmacies under multiple unit organization are typical of densely populated, high income areas.

Economic characteristics are not the only variables affecting the structure of the market. Four types of regulation impact on market structure:

1. Advertising Restrictions
2. Physical Requirements for Establishments
3. Pharmacist Ownership Requirements
4. Regulation of Competing Distribution Methods

Restrictions on the ability of pharmacies to advertise or promote prescription drug prices are associated with a larger number of small volume relatively inefficient size pharmacies. The substantive effect of these regulations on establishment sales size is excessive distribution costs and waste.

Regulations specifying the allocation of pharmacies available physical resources (floor space or entrance for example) serve to reduce the ability to expand nonprescription product lines. Consequently pharmacies in states regulating the physical characteristics of establishments have higher ratios of prescription sales to total sales than pharmacies in unregulated states. As a result, these establishments have higher average costs than pharmacies in states where this type of regulation has not been implemented.

The requirement for pharmacist ownership of pharmacies is associated with a relative infrequent observation of establishments under chain organization. Members of pharmacy boards commonly voice the opinion (which is probably correct) that chain organization management has a more mercantile orientation toward pharmacy practice than independent owner pharmacists.[2] In states limiting pharmacy ownership to pharmacists, informal standards mandating a "professional" orientation, and manifest as low volume, high margin prescription-oriented establishments, are more easily maintained. While there is no direct impact on operating costs associated with limited chain store organization, economies in purchasing and coordination associated with chain operations are reflected in lower prescription drug prices.

The overall effect of these three types of regulation on market structure is the maintenance of a relatively homogeneous pattern of low volume prescription-oriented pharmacies. The fourth type of regulation associated with market structure displays an exceptional relationship to this pattern.

Regulations enacted which limit the distribution of prescription drugs to retail pharmacies and prevent distribution through mail order firms or prescription agents, or regulations which prohibit the sale of proprietary drugs in vending machines are associated with a relatively higher proportion of pharmacies under chain organization. Fletcher concludes that such regulations have been enacted as a result of the growth of chains and therefore represent an attempt by regulators to limit any further sources of competition to independent pharmacies. An alternative explanation may be that the limitation of drug distribution to pharmacies provides a strong economic incentive (in the absence of formal or informal proscriptions) to expand into chain organization and obtain the benefits of purchasing and coordination offered by this organizational form.

Although regulation, in the main, is associated with a relatively inefficient supply structure the trend toward larger and more diversified pharmacies is still very much apparent. Thus it appears that while regulation may effectively impede the process of evolution in market structure it is obvious that such change cannot be forestalled indefinitely. The substantial economic incentives for growth and diversification have led to challenges to regulatory authority, frequently resulting in a demise of regulatory impact in the market.

Structure and Conduct

The retail prescription drug market is characterized by a good deal of diversity in price and nonprice offer variation among establishments. Price levels and variation in the provision of services are closely related to structural characteristics.

The analysis presented in Chapter 7 strongly suggests that by virtue of distinct differences in market offerings the retail prescription drug market is comprised of three primary components.

1. *The mass market.* Served primarily by large chain-owned pharmacies offering a wide assortment of nonprescription products priced at discount, low prescription prices, and relatively few general or professional services. These pharmacies offer long hours of operation, Sunday and holiday operating hours. Their location in shopping centers makes them easily accessible on shopping trips.

2. *The service component.* Served by pharmacies of intermediate volume. These pharmacies offer less product variety than those serving the mass market and less frequently discount nonprescription products. Their real distinction is in the provision of a variety of general and professional services.

3. *The local market.* Served typically by small volume independent prescription specialists. Typically these pharmacies do not offer the same range of services as pharmacies supplying the service component. Product assortment is limited and seldom discounted. Prescription prices are highest for these pharmacies. Located in residential areas (but not in shopping centers) or in medical buildings these pharmacies rely heavily on the benefits of locational monopoly.

Regulation and Conduct

The regulation most directly affecting competitive conduct is a restriction on prescription price advertising. In the absence of price information, consumers must make the choice of a pharmacy on some basis other than explicitly provided price information. The limited availability of price information serves to decrease the propensity of consumers to switch from one type of pharmacy offer package to another. Outlet loyalty develops on the basis of nonprice offer variations. The relatively high cost of search for lower prices in the uninformed market serves to decrease price elasticity, increase outlet loyalty, and decrease the rate of change in supply structure resulting from any changes in consumer preferences.

In states where advertising is permitted, price becomes an active rather than a passive element in the mix of offer variations. Pharmacy management must adjust the mix of merchandise, services, and prices to meet consumer preferences. Given the relatively low cost of providing some services pharmacies in unregulated states across size classifications display insignificant differences in service levels when other variables are controlled for. Minimal standards of service reach a type of equilibrium level. Price competition serves to reduce the level and dispersion of prescription drug prices. In neither regulated nor unregulated states does competition result in uniform prescription drug prices, but rather results in variability in prices reflecting the composition of the market offer of each pharmacy.

In summary:

1. Service *levels* are approximately the same in states regulating advertising and in states permitting advertising.
2. *Variations* in services among size classifications are greater in states regulating advertising than in states permitting advertising.
3. Prescription price *levels* are higher in states regulating advertising than in states permitting advertising.
4. *Variations* in prescription prices are greater in states regulating advertising than in states permitting advertising.

Performance—Conclusions and
Implications

Regulation of the retail distribution of prescription drugs results in significant economic effects. These effects are manifest as excessive distribution costs—borne by society at large, and monopoly prices—borne solely by prescription drug purchasers. Table 9-1 presents the estimates of structural costs of regulation developed in Chapter 5 and the price effects developed in Chapter 8.

Table 9-1
Economic Impact of Retail Prescription Drug Market Regulation (1970)

Impact	Low Estimate	High Estimate
Distribution costs	$ 63,000,000	$ 66,000,000
Prescription prices	157,000,000	176,000,000
Total	$220,000,000	$242,000,000

The total economic impact of regulation is between $220 and $242 million dollars in 1970. These figures represent approximately 5 percent of prescription sales in that year. A similar figure based on 1973 estimates of prescription drug sales would be in the neighborhood of $400 million dollars.

In terms of regulations contributing to this economic impact the regulation of prescription drug price advertising is, by far, the most significant. Not only does this regulation affect market structure and result in excessive costs, but it also results in prices significantly above average costs. Average prices are higher and the dispersion of prescription prices greater in states regulating price advertising. It is significant to note that regulations restricting price advertising of prescription drugs have been the primary focus of current critics of retail pharmacy regulation. If alleviation of the bulk of the economic consequences of regulation is the purpose of these critics then this emphasis on advertising regulations is not misplaced.

Two issues remain standing. These are: (1) the effectiveness of retail pharmacy regulation in promoting and maintaining public health and safety; (2) recommendations to policymakers as to appropriate action regarding pharmacy regulation. These two issues are intrinsically tied together for the dual role for public policy in this market is a provision for public health and safety as well as maintenance of an efficient system for the distribution of prescription drug products.

Conclusions regarding maintenance of public health and safety in the absence of regulation may be made only inferentially, but two points deserve mention. First, this study did not address itself to professional pharmacy licensing per se. It was assumed that licensing of pharmacists and mandating professional standards of competence were legitimate and socially supported functions of pharmacy boards. In this regard, the professional standards maintained by pharmacists in training and practice may be, in themselves, sufficient to protect the public from detrimental trade practices. Second, one measure of professional performance is the level of professional services provided by pharmacies. As shown in this study service levels are structurally related and largely unaffected by regulation. This conclusion denotes that there is a demand for professional services by a substantial segment of prescription drug purchasers. Furthermore it infers that a professional and mercantile orientation to pharmacy practice (if by professional is meant the provision of services, and by mercantile is meant efficient pharmacy management) are not irreconcilable nor are they even incompatible. Retail pharmacies are able to perform efficiently while at the same time providing professional services.

These conclusions are presented to public policymakers and this study assumes its objective of providing a feedback mechanism. The economic costs of regulation of the retail prescription drug market are not insignificant. These costs result primarily from the regulation of prescription drug price advertising. While it may conceivably be shown that there are benefits to be derived from this type of regulation equalling or even surpassing the costs estimated in this study, no one has yet pointed them out.

The question of what to do about currently existing regulation depends precisely on the evaluation of policymakers of the tradeoff between the economic costs of regulation and potential benefits. What this study clearly indicates is that before public agencies are mobilized for the initiation of further regulation sound prospective analysis is required.[a] It would be surprising indeed to find proposed regulation not to be in the economic best interest of those who espouse it.

---

[a]The National Association of Retail Druggists and the American Pharmaceutical Association recently proposed that a variety of "over-the-counter" drugs should be sold only by pharmacists. These drugs would include certain cold and cough remedies and antacids among others. Several pharmacy boards are considering proposals requiring pharmacies to maintain family prescription records.

Appendix

Appendix

This Appendix lists the states having the regulations listed in Chapter 2.

1. *Ownership Prohibitions*
   California, Colorado, Maryland, Mississippi, Pennsylvania, Utah

2. *Ownership Requirements*
   Michigan, Montana, North Dakota, South Dakota

3. *Merchandising Prohibitions*
   Maine, Minnesota

4. *No Permit for Fair Trade Violator*
   Mississippi

5. *Limitation on Outlets*
   Arkansas

6. *Physical Separation for Prescription Department*
   Arkansas, Connecticut, Delaware, Indiana, Kansas, Michigan, Minnesota, Montana, New York, Pennsylvania, South Dakota, Virginia

7. *Separate Entrance Mandatory*
   Kansas, Maine, Minnesota, Montana, Pennsylvania, Utah, Virginia

8. *Entrance to Adjoining Store Prohibited*
   Maine

9. *Minimum Floor Space Requirement for Pharmacy Department*
   California, Delaware, Louisiana, Massachusetts, Minnesota, Mississippi, Montana, New Jersey, New Mexico, Oklahoma, Pennsylvania, Rhode Island, Wisconsin

10. *Self-Service for Nonprescription Products Prohibited*
    Minnesota, South Dakota, Wisconsin

11. *Minimum Prescription Inventory Requirement*
    Indiana, Mississippi

12. *Ban on "Closed Door" Operations*
    Florida, Maryland, Massachusetts, Mississippi, Pennsylvania, South Carolina

13. *Outdoor Signs Controlled*
    Michigan, New Jersey

14. *Prohibition on Implying Discount Prescription Prices*
    California, Colorado, Louisiana, Maine, Maryland, Massachusetts, Mississippi, New Jersey, New York, Pennsylvania

15. *Advertising Prescription Prices Prohibited*

Arkansas, Colorado, Connecticut, Florida, Georgia, Illinois, Indiana, Iowa, Kansas, Louisiana, Maine, Maryland, Massachusetts, Michigan, Minnesota, Nevada, New Jersey, New York, Oklahoma, Oregon, Pennsylvania, Rhode Island, South Dakota, Texas, Virginia, Washington, West Virginia, Wisconsin

16. *Promotional Schemes Prohibited*

Colorado, Michigan, New Jersey, Pennsylvania, Virginia

17. *Pharmacist Manager Requirement*

Alaska, Colorado, Connecticut, Maryland, Massachusetts, New Jersey, New York, Ohio, Oklahoma, Oregon, Pennsylvania, Tennessee, Vermont, Virginia, West Virginia, Wisconsin

18. *Pharmacist on Duty When Store Is Open*

Alaska, Arizona, Connecticut, Massachusetts, Michigan, Minnesota, Montana, New Hampshire, New York, Oregon, Pennsylvania, Rhode Island, Tennessee, Virginia, Wisconsin

19. *Specification of Hours for Pharmacy to Be Open*
Massachusetts

20. *Specification of Hours Worked by Pharmacists*

Arkansas, Colorado, Kentucky, Massachusetts, Minnesota, Montana, New York

21. *Specification of Number of Pharmacists Employed*
Alabama, New Hampshire, Pennsylvania

22. *Prescription Dispensing Rules*

California, Colorado, Illinois, Indiana, Iowa, Kansas, Louisiana, Virginia

23. *No Prescription Agents*

Alabama, Arkansas, California, Colorado, Florida, Georgia, Kansas, Louisiana, Maine, Massachusetts, Mississippi, Ohio, Oklahoma, Pennsylvania, Rhode Island, Washington

24. *Mail Order Drug Sales Prohibited*

Arizona, California, Florida, Illinois, Massachusetts, Michigan, Minnesota, Mississippi, Nevada, New Mexico, Ohio, Oklahoma, Oregon, Pennsylvania, South Dakota, Tennessee, Washington

25. *Ban on Vending Machine Sale of Proprietaries*

Arizona, Arkansas, California, Colorado, Connecticut, Georgia, Idaho, Indiana, Iowa, Louisiana, Maryland, Minnesota, Montana, New Hampshire, New Mexico, North Dakota, Ohio, Oregon, Utah, Virginia, Washington, West Virginia, Wisconsin

Notes

Notes

Notes To Chapter 1
Introduction

1. B.S. Cooper and Nancy Worthington, *National Health Expenditures, Calendar Years 1929-1970*, U.S. Department of Health, Education and Welfare Research and Statistics Note No. 1 (Washington: U.S. Government Printing Office, 1972), p. 4.

2. Benjamin Rosenthal, *Retail Prescription Drug Prices*, U.S. Congress, House Document, March 19, 1973, p. 1880.

3. U.S. Social Security Administration, *Prescription Drug Data Summary* (Washington: U.S. Government Printing Office, 1972), p. 8.

4. U.S. Department of Health, Education and Welfare, *Task Force on Prescription Drugs: Final Report* (Washington: U.S. Government Printing Office, 1969), p. 2.

5. U.S. Department of Health, Education and Welfare, *Task Force on Prescription Drugs: Second Interim Report and Recommendations* (Washington: U.S. Government Printing Office, 1968), p. 4.

6. Roland Donnem, "Federal Antitrust Law Versus Anti Competitive State Regulation," An address before The Sherman Act Committee of the Anti-Trust Section of the American Bar Association, St. Louis, Missouri, August 10, 1970, pp. 5-6.

7. Letter from Caspar W. Weinberger, Chairman, Federal Trade Commission to Dwight A. Ink, Assistant Director, Office of Executive Management, Bureau of the Budget, May 20, 1970.

8. Letter from Richard G. Kleindienst, Deputy Attorney General, Department of Justice to Robert P. Mayo, Director Bureau of the Budget, March, 1970.

9. Rosenthal, *Retail Prescription*, p. 1879.

10. Ibid., p. 1889.

11. *Prescription Drug Price Survey (Preliminary Survey)*, California Legislature Assembly Office of Research (Sacramento, California, April, 1973). (mimeographed).

12. M. McColgan, State Legislature—*House Bill No. 2013*, The Commonwealth of Massachusetts (Boston, 1973).

13. R.A. Borten, Executive Director, Boston Consumers' Council, *The Report on the Effect of Boston's Drug Price Posting Regulation* (Boston, 1972). (mimeographed).

14. Dan Kushner, "Mandatory Prescription Pricing: New York Next?" *American Druggist* (February 21, 1972), pp. 18-21.

15. Consumer Council of the Genessee Valley, Inc., *Consumer Comment* (Genessee Valley, New York: Consumer Council of the Genessee Valley, Inc., June, 1972), Vol. 3, Issue 6.

16. Borten, *Report on Boston.*

17. Stephanie Russell, Spokeswoman for Women for Political and Social Action, *Findings and Recommendations of the Department on Consumer Affairs and Board of Pharmacy Informal Hearings on Advertisement of Prescription Drugs* (Sacramento, California: undated), p. 1. (mimeograph)

18. Alfonso Baez, Spokesman for Chicanos for Creative Medicine, *Findings and Recommendations of the Department on Consumer Affairs and Board of Pharmacy Informal Hearings on Advertisement of Prescription Drugs* (Sacramento, California: undated), p. 1.

19. Kushner, "Mandatory Prescription Pricing."

20. Borten, *Report on Boston.*

21. Sylvester Berki, *Prescription Dispensing in Twenty Pharmacies: Characteristics, Utilizers, Services and Costs* (Ann Arbor, Michigan: The University of Michigan School of Public Health, January, 1971). (mimeographed).

Notes to Chapter 2
Public Policy and the Retail Market
for Prescription Drugs

1. J. Boddewyn and S.C. Hollander, *Public Policy Toward Retailing* (Lexington, Massachusetts: Lexington Books, D.C. Heath and Company, 1972), p. 1.

2. Thomas R. Dye, "A Model for the Analysis of Policy Outcomes," in Ira Sharkansky (ed.), *Policy Analysis in Political Science* (Chicago, Illinois: Markham Publishing Co., 1972).

3. J.B. Blake (ed.), *Safeguarding the Public: Historical Aspects of Medicinal Drug Control* (Baltimore, Maryland: The Johns Hopkins Press, 1970).

4. Pennsylvania, *Annotated Statutes*, 6 3 C. 9 (1959), and, (1965 Supplement), Sect. 390-4(j).

5. A good source of these statutes in summarized form is: F. Marion Fletcher, *Market Restraints in the Retail Drug Industry* (Philadelphia, Pennsylvania: University of Pennsylvania Press, 1967).

6. For examples in other areas of trade see: Stanley C. Hollander, *Restraints Upon Retail Competition*, Marketing and Transportation Paper No. 14, Bureau of Business and Economic Research (East Lansing, Michigan: Michigan State University, 1965).

7. Fletcher, *Market Restraints*, p. 39.

8. Ibid., p. 40.

9. Ibid., pp. 40-45.

10. Ibid., pp. 50-51.

11. *Facts on N.A.R.D.* (Chicago, Illinois: National Association of Retail Druggists, 1965), p. 2.

12. J.C. Palamountain, *The Politics of Distribution* (Cambridge, Massachusetts: Harvard University Press, 1955), p. 94.

13. *This Is Your Opportunity to Associate, Again* (Washington, D.C.: National Association of Chain Drug Stores, 1965), p. 4.

14. Fletcher, *Market Restraints*, Chapter 7; and, Palamountain, *Politics of Distribution.*

15. Fletcher, *Market Restraints*, p. 207.

16. P. Bucklin, *Competition and Evolution in the Distributive Trades* (Englewood Cliffs, New Jersey: Prentice-Hall, Inc., 1972), p. 281.

17. These issues may be studied in the following sources: (A) *Findings and Recommendations of the Department of Consumer Affairs and Board of Pharmacy Informal Hearings on Advertisement of Prescription Drugs* (Sacramento, California: undated). (mimeograph); (B) Benjamin Rosenthal, *Retail Prescription Drug Prices*, U.S., Congress, House Document, March 9, 1973; (C) Fletcher, *Market Restraints.*

18. J.M. Carman, "Theories to Describe Some Environmental Conditions in Which the Firm Operates," A paper presented at the Fall Educators Conference of the American Marketing Association, August 1973, p. 3.

19. Ibid., pp. 6-7.

20. L.P. Bucklin and J.M. Carman, "Vertical Market Structure Theory and the Health Care Delivery System," in Jagdish N. Sheth and Peter L. Wright (eds.), *Marketing Analysis for Societal Problems* (Urbana-Champaign, Illinois: University of Illinois, 1974).

21. Carman, "Theories to Describe Environmental Conditions," p. 7.

22. Edward Chamberlin, *The Theory of Monopolistic Competition* (6 ed., 1970; Cambridge, Massachusetts; Harvard University Press, 1933), pp. 82-83.

23. Ibid., p. 95.

Notes to Chapter 3
An Overview of the Market

1. These categories are outlined in F.M. Fletcher, *Market Restraints in the Retail Drug Industry* (Philadelphia, Pennsylvania: University of Pennsylvania Press, 1967).

2. U.S. Bureau of the Census, *Census of Business: Retail Trade*, I, 1967. This definition includes drugstores and proprietary stores.

3. Douglas J. Dalrymple and Donald L. Thompson, *Retailing: An Economic View* (New York: The Free Press, 1969), p. 14.

4. *The Lilly Digest* (Indianapolis, Indiana: Eli Lilly and Company, 1972).

5. Louis P. Bucklin and Michael Etgar, "The Proprietary Drugs Market," unpublished paper, The University of California, Berkeley, 1972.

Notes to Chapter 4
Cost Function and the Cost Structure
of Pharmacy Retailing

1. For a comprehensive treatment of these problems see: Edna Douglas, "Size of Firm and Structure of Costs in Retailing," *Journal of Business* 35 (April 1962): 158-190. J. Johnston, *Statistical Cost Analysis* (New York: McGraw-Hill, 1960), David Schwartzman, *The Decline of Service in Retail Trade: An Analysis of the Growth of Sales per Manhour, 1929-1963* (Pullman, Washington: Bureau of Economic and Business Research Study No. 48, June 1971), especially pp. 105-115.

2. Douglas, "Size of Firm," pp. 159-160, and Bob R. Holdren, *The Structure of a Retail Market and the Market Behavior of Retail Units* (Englewood Cliffs, New Jersey: Prentice-Hall, 1960), pp. 27-28.

3. See: Joel Dean, "Department Store Cost Functions," in Oscar Longe et al. (eds.), *Studies in Mathematical Economics and Econometrics* (Chicago, Illinois: University of Chicago Press, 1942), pp. 222-254.

4. Douglas, "Size of Firm," p. 160.

5. Ibid.

6. Milton Friedman, "Comment," *Business Concentration and Price Policy* (Princeton, New Jersey: Princeton University Press, 1955), pp. 230-238.

7. Johnston, *Statistical Cost Analysis.*

8. Reprinted from Edna Douglas "Size of Firm and Structure of Costs in Retailing," *Journal of Business* 35 (April 1962): 160-161 by permission of the University of Chicago Press. Copyright 1962 by the University of Chicago.

9. Johnston, *Statistical Cost Analysis.*

10. These surveys are published annually as *The Lilly Digest*, a survey of independent community pharmacy operations and *The N.A.C.D.S.–Lilly Digest*, a survey of chain pharmacy operations.

11. The long-run average cost function described is one consistently found in empirical cost studies. See for example, J. Johnston, *Statistical Cost Analysis* (New York: McGraw-Hill, 1960); and Joel Dean, "Statistical Cost Functions for a Hosiery Mill," in Edwin Mansfield (ed.), *Micro-Economics: Selected Readings* (New York: W.W. Norton and Company, 1971), pp. 115-124.

12. Holdren, *Structure of a Retail Market*, p. 33.

Note to Chapter 5
Structural Effects and Structural
Costs of Regulation

1. Marion Fletcher, *Market Restraints in the Retail Drug Industry* (Philadelphia, Pennsylvania: University of Pennsylvania Press, 1967).

Notes to Chapter 7
Regulation and Competition:
Dimensions of Nonprice and Price
Offer Variations

1. Paul E. Nelson and Lee E. Preston, *Price Merchandising in Food Retailing: A Case Study* (Berkeley, California: IBER Special Publications, 1966).

2. Tibor Scitovsky, *Welfare and Competition: The Economics of a Fully Employed Economy* (Chicago, Illinois: Richard D. Irwin, 1951).

3. William Baumol, "Calculation of Optimal Product and Retailer Characteristics: The Abstract Product Approach," *The Journal of Political Economy* 75, 5 (University of Chicago Press, 1967), pp. 674-685.

4. Ibid., p. 674. By permission of the University of Chicago Press, Copyright 1967 by the University of Chicago.

5. Bob R. Holdren, *The Structure of a Retail Market and the Behavior of Retail Units* (Englewood Cliffs, New Jersey: Prentice-Hall, 1960). See especially Chapter 6.

6. The physical size categories contained in the N.A.R.D./N.A.C.D.S. Survey are used for this variable. The variable is thus ordinal in nature. The use of this variable in this form does not affect the results of the analysis. See Harry C. Triandis, *Attitude and Attitude Change* (New York: John Wiley and Sons, 1971), p. 38, and the references contained therein.

7. Two excellent discussions of the discriminant analysis model may be found in: W.W. Cooley and P.R. Lohnes, *Multivariate Data Analysis* (New York: John Wiley and Sons, 1971), Chapter 9; and Maurice Tatsuoka, *Multivariate Analysis: Techniques for Educational and Psychological Research* (New York: John Wiley and Sons, 1971), Chapter 6.

8. See, for example Paul E. Green and Vithala R. Rao, *Applied Multidimensional Scaling* (New York: Holt, Rinehart and Winston, Inc., 1972).

9. See Tatsuoka, *Multivariate Analysis*, pp. 164-165. If the number of significant discriminant functions thus found is smaller than the number of possible discriminant functions $r = \min(k - 1, p)$ a further reduction in dimensionality required to describe the differences among the k groups has been effected.

Notes to Chapter 8
Regulation and Prescription Drug
Prices

1. Lee Benham, "The Effect of Advertising on the Price of Eyeglasses," *Journal of Law and Economics* 15, 2 (October 1972): 345-46.

2. Variables representing geographic location are dummy variables representing one of nine Census regions.

Census Region I:	Connecticut, Maine, Massachusetts, New Hampshire, Rhode Island, Vermont
Census Region II:	New Jersey, New York, Pennsylvania
Census Region III:	District of Columbia, Delaware, Florida, Georgia, Maryland, North Carolina, South Carolina, Virginia, West Virginia
Census Region IV:	Illinois, Indiana, Michigan, Ohio, Wisconsin
Census Region V:	Alabama, Kentucky, Mississippi, Tennessee
Census Region VI:	Iowa, Kansas, Minnesota, Missouri, Nebraska, North Dakota, South Dakota
Census Region VII:	Arkansas, Louisiana, Oklahoma, Texas
Census Region VIII:	Arizona, Colorado, Idaho, Montana, Nevada, New Mexico, Utah, Wyoming
Census Region IX:	California, Oregon, Washington

3. This apparently is the interpretation Fletcher puts to such findings. See F. Marion Fletcher, *Market Restrictions in the Retail Drug Industry* (Philadelphia, Pennsylvania: University of Pennsylvania Press, 1967), p. 289.

4. U.S., Social Security Administration, *Prescription Drug Data Summary* (Washington, U.S. Government Printing Office, 1972), pp. 4, 6.

Notes to Chapter 9
Summary and Implications

1. Louis P. Bucklin, *Competition and Evolution in the Distributive Trades* (Englewood Cliffs, New Jersey: Prentice-Hall, 1972), p. 141.

2. F. Marion Fletcher, *Market Restraints in the Retail Drug Industry* (Philadelphia, Pennsylvania, University of Pennsylvania Press, 1967), p. 290.

Bibliography

Bibliography

Books and Monographs

Alderson, Wroe and Miller, N.A. *Costs, Sales, and Profits in the Retail Drug Store.* U.S. Foreign and Domestic Commerce Bureau, No. 90. Washington, D.C.: U.S. Government Printing Office, 1932.

Assael, Henry (ed.). *The Politics of Distributive Trade Associations: A Study of Conflict Resolution.* Hempsted, New York: Hofstra University Yearbook in Business Series 4, 1967.

Berki, Sylvester. *Prescription Dispensing in Twenty Pharmacies, Utilizers, Services and Costs.* Ann Arbor, Michigan: The University of Michigan School of Public Health, 1971.

Blake, J.B. (ed.). *Safeguarding the Public: Historical Aspects of Medicinal Drug Control.* Baltimore, Maryland: The Johns Hopkins Press, 1970.

Boddewyn, J.J. and Hollander, S.C. (eds.). *Public Policy Toward Retailing.* Lexington, Massachusetts: Lexington Books, D.C. Heath and Company, 1972.

Bucklin, Louis P. *Competition and Evolution in the Distributive Trades.* Englewood Cliffs, New Jersey: Prentice-Hall, Inc., 1972.

Bucklin, L.P. and Etgar, Michael. *The Proprietary Drugs Market.* Berkeley, California: 1972 mimeograph.

Burley, O.E., Fisher, A.B., and Cox, R.G. *Drug Store Operating Costs and Profits.* New York: McGraw-Hill Book Company, 1956.

Chamberlin, Edward. *The Theory of Monopolistic Competition.* Cambridge, Massachusetts: Harvard University Press, 1970.

Cooley, W.W. and Lohnes, P.R. *Multivariate Data Analysis.* New York: John Wiley and Sons, 1971.

Cooper, B.S. and Worthington, Nancy. *National Health Expenditures, Calendar Years 1929-1970.* Washington, D.C.: U.S. Government Printing Office Research and Statistics Note No. 1, 1972.

Dalrymple, Douglas and Thompson, Donald L. *Retailing, An Economic View.* New York: The Free Press, 1969.

Firestone, John M. *Trends in Prescription Drug Prices.* Washington, D.C.: American Enterprise Institute for Public Policy Research, 1970.

Fletcher, F. Marion. *Market Restraints in the Retail Drug Industry.* Philadelphia, Pennsylvania: University of Pennsylvania Press, 1967.

Green, Paul E. and Rao, Vithala. *Applied Multidimensional Scaling: A Comparison of Approaches and Algorithms.* New York: Holt, Rinehart and Winston, 1972.

Hall, Margaret, Knapp, J., and Winston, C. *Distribution in Great Britain and North America.* London: Oxford University Press, 1961.

Holdren, Bob R. *The Structure of a Retail Market and the Market Behavior of Retail Units.* Englewood Cliffs, New Jersey: Prentice-Hall, 1960.

Hollander, Stanley C. *Restraints Upon Retail Competition.* East Lansing, Michigan: Michigan State University Bureau of Business and Economic Research, Marketing and Transportation Paper No. 14, 1965.

Johnston, J. *Statistical Cost Analysis.* New York: McGraw-Hill Book Company, 1960.

Myers, Robert J. *Coverage of Out-Of-Hospital Prescription Drugs Under Medicare.* Washington, D.C.: American Enterprise Institute for Public Policy Research, 1972.

Nelson, P.E. and Preston, L.E. *Price Merchandising in Food Retailing: A Case Study.* Berkeley, California: IBER Special Publication, 1966.

Palamountain, J.C. *The Politics of Distribution.* Cambridge, Massachusetts: Harvard University Press, 1955.

Scitovsky, Tibor. *Welfare and Competition: The Economics of a Fully Employed Economy.* Chicago, Illinois: Richard D. Irwin, 1951.

Sheth, Jagdish N. and Wright, Peter L. (eds.). *Marketing Analysis for Societal Problems.* Urbana-Champaign, Illinois: University of Illinois, 1974.

Tatsuoka, Maurice. *Multivariate Data Analysis: Techniques for Educational and Psychological Research.* New York: John Wiley and Sons, 1971.

Triandis, Harry C. *Attitude and Attitude Change.* New York: John Wiley and Sons, 1971.

Van Tassel, Charles E. *An Analysis of Factors Influencing Retail Sales.* East Lansing, Michigan: Michigan State University Press, 1966.

Walker, Hugh D. *Market Power and Price Levels in the Ethical Drug Industry.* Bloomington, Indiana: Indiana University Press, 1971.

Articles and Presentations

Baumol, William. "Calculation of Optimal Product and Retailer Characteristics: The Abstract Product Approach." *The Journal of Political Economy* 75, 5 (October 1967).

Benham, Lee. "The Effect of Advertising on the Price of Eyeglasses." *Journal of Law and Economics* 15, 2 (October 1972).

Boddewyn, J. and Hollander, S.C. "Public Policies Toward Retailing Around the World." *Proceedings of the Fall Educators Conference, 1973.* American Marketing Association, Chicago, Illinois, 1974.

Carmen, J.M. "Theories to Describe Some Environmental Conditions in Which the Firm Operates." A paper presented to the Fall Educators Conference, American Marketing Association, August 1973.

Dean, Joel. "Department Store Cost Functions." In Oscar Longe et al. (eds.), *Studies in Mathematical Economics and Econometrics.* Chicago, Illinois: The University of Chicago Press, 1942.

Dean, Joel. "Statistical Cost Function for a Hosiery Mill." In Edwin Mansfield (ed.), *Microeconomics: Selected Readings*. New York: W.W. Norton and Company, 1971.

Donnem, Roland. "Federal Antitrust Law Versus Anti Competitive State Regulation." Paper delivered before The Sherman Act Committee, American Bar Association, St. Louis, Missouri, August 1970.

Douglas, Edna. "Size of Firm and Structure of Costs in Retailing." *Journal of Business* 35 (April 1972).

Dye, Thomas R. "A Model for the Analysis of Policy Outcomes." In Ira Sharkansky (ed.), *Policy Analysis in Political Science*. Chicago, Illinois: Markham Publishing Company, 1972.

Engman, Lewis A. Untitled paper presented before the Annual Meeting of the Antitrust Law Section, American Bar Association, Honolulu, Hawaii, August 1974.

Friedman, Milton. "Comment." *Business Concentration and Price Policy*. Princeton, New Jersey: Princeton University Press, 1955.

Green, James. "Welfare Losses From Monopoly In The Drug Industry: The Oklahoma 'Antisubstitution' Law." *Antitrust Law and Economics Review* 5, 3 (Spring 1972).

Kushner, D. "Mandatory Prescription Pricing: New York Next?" *American Druggist*, (February 1972).

"Prescription Drugs—The War Over Secret Prices." *Changing Times* (February 1973).

Stigler, George. "The Theory of Economic Regulation." *The Bell Journal of Economics and Management Science*, (Autumn 1971).

Wiegel, William F. "State Legislation Restricting the Sale of Drugs." *Food Drug Cosmetic Law Journal* 13, 1 (January 1958).

Unauthored Reports

Consumer Comment. Consumer Council of the Genessee Valley, Inc., Vol. 3, Issue 6, June, 1972.

Facts on N.A.R.D. Chicago, Illinois: National Association of Retail Druggists, 1965.

Findings and Recommendations of the Department on Consumer Affairs and Board of Pharmacy Informal Hearings on Advertisement of Prescription Drugs. Sacramento, California, undated.

N.A.C.D.S.–Lilly Digest 1971. Indianapolis, Indiana: Eli Lilly and Company, 1971.

Prescription Drug Price Survey (Preliminary Survey). Sacramento, California: California Legislature Assembly Office of Research, April, 1973.

Sales Management: The Marketing Magazine. 1971 Survey of Buying Power. New York: Sales Management Inc., July 10, 1971.

The Lilly Digest. Indianapolis, Indiana: Eli Lilly and Company, 1971, 1972.
This Is Your Opportunity to Associate, Again. Washington, D.C.: National Association of Chain Drug Stores, 1954.

Government Documents

U.S. Bureau of the Census. *Census of Business: Retail Trade,* 1967.
U.S. Department of Health, Education and Welfare. *Task Force on Prescription Drugs: Final Report,* 1969.
U.S. Department of Health, Education and Welfare. *Task Force on Prescription Drugs: Second Interim Report and Recommendations,* 1968.
U.S. Social Security Administration. *Prescription Drug Data Summary,* 1972.

Special Documents

Borten, R.A. *The Report on the Effect of Boston's Drug Price Posting Regulation.* Boston, Massachusetts, 1972.
McColgan, M. *House Bill No. 2013.* The Commonwealth of Massachusetts, 1973.
Rosenthal, Benjamin (Hon.). *Retail Prescription Drug Prices.* U.S. Congress, House Document, March 19, 1973.
Virginia Citizens Consumer Council, et al. v. State Board of Pharmacy, et al. Civil No. 73-336-R. U.S. District Ct. Eastern District Va. March 21, 1974.

Correspondence

Kleindienst, Richard G., Deputy Attorney General, Department of Justice to Mayo, Robert P., Director, Bureau of the Budget, March 1970.
Weinberger, Casper W., Chairman, Federal Trade Commission to Ink, Dwight, Assistant Director, Office of Executive Management, Bureau of the Budget, May 1970.

Index

Index

About the Author

John F. Cady is assistant professor of marketing, College of Business and Public Administration, The University of Arizona. He is a graduate of the School of Management, State University of New York at Buffalo.

He is a member of the American Marketing Association and The American Council on Consumer Interests. His previous research deals with marketing and public policy, and marketing and social issues. He has contributed to the *Journal of Consumer Affairs* and the *Journal of Allied Health.*